The Complete Rice Cooker Cookbook

Over 100 recipes for breakfast, main dishes, soups, and desserts

By Susan Evans

Copyright © 2015 Susan Evans

All rights reserved. This book or any portion thereof may not be reproduced or used in any manner whatsoever without the express written permission of the publisher except for the use of brief quotations in a book review.

Other popular books by Susan Evans

Vegetarian Mediterranean Cookbook:
Over 50 recipes for appetizers, salads, dips, and main dishes

Quick & Easy Asian Vegetarian Cookbook:
Over 50 recipes for stir fries, rice, noodles, and appetizers

Vegetarian Slow Cooker Cookbook:
Over 75 recipes for meals, soups, stews, desserts, and sides

Quick & Easy Vegan Desserts Cookbook:
Over 80 delicious recipes for cakes, cupcakes, brownies, cookies, fudge, pies, candy, and so much more!

Quick & Easy Microwave Meals:
Over 50 recipes for breakfast, snacks, meals and desserts

Halloween Cookbook:
80 Ghoulish recipes for appetizers, meals, drinks, and desserts

FREE BONUS!

Would you like to receive one of my cookbooks for free? Just leave me on honest review on Amazon and I will send you a digital version of the cookbook of your choice! All you have to do is email me proof of your review and the desired cookbook and format to susan.evans.author@gmail.com. Thank you for your support, and have fun cooking!

Measurement Conversions 1

Introduction 2

Rice Cooker Meals Cookbook 3

Breakfast 4

Avocado Breakfast Bowl 5
Rice Cooker Oatmeal 6
Coconut Tapioca Pudding 7
Quick and Easy Oats 8
Steel Cut Oatmeal 9
Frittata in a Rice Cooker 10
Tapioca Pudding 11

Chicken Rice Dishes 12

Spinach, Mushroom, and Chicken Risotto 13
Garlic Chicken Fragrant Rice 14
Oriental Chicken and Rice 15
Yellow Chicken Flavored Rice 16
Curry Chicken Jambalaya 17
Sesame Chicken Rice 18
Ginger Chicken and Rice 19
Rice, Artichoke, Spinach, and Chicken Salad 20

SEAFOOD RICE DISHES 22

Cajun Crawfish Tails with Rice 23
Shrimp Jambalaya 24
Salmon Risotto with Rice 25
Seafood Jambalaya 26
Easy Rice-Cooker Shrimp Jambalaya 27

RED MEAT RICE DISHES 28

Bacon Fried Rice 29
Jambalaya Sausage with Beans 30
Chinese Sausage and Rice 31
Jambalaya with Sausage 32
Bacon and Onion Rice 33
Rice-Cooker Jambalaya 34

OTHER RICE DISHES 35

Mexican Rice 36
Dill and Lemon Rice with Feta 37
Cajun Wild Rice 38
Chile Cheese Rice 39
Caribbean Rice 40
Rice and Lentils 41
Easy Risotto 42
Saffron & Fruit Chutney Yellow Rice 43
Rice and Black Beans 44

NON-RICE DISHES 45

Curried Squash and Pork..46
Very Cheesy Polenta..47
Paprika Chicken...48
Pasta Cubano...49
Potato Salad..50
Roasted Pork...51
Soy Chicken...52
Quinoa Pomegranate salad..53
Super Cheesy Polenta...54
Steamed Tofu & Asparagus 55
Creamy Macaroni and Cheese.......................................56
Chicken Quinoa with Sun-dried Tomatoes 57
Cheesy Mac and Cheese...58
Rice Cooker Quinoa 59
Healthy Rice-Cooker Barley 60
Romano Cheese Pasta..61
Meat Cabbage Casserole..62

SOUPS AND STEWS........................63

Rice and Beef Soup 64
Taco Soup 65
Chicken Chili...66
Turkey Barley Goulash Casserole 67
Chicken & White Radish Soup 68

DESSERTS..69

Coconut-Pecan Upside Down Cake..............................70

Chocolate Cake 71
Muffin Cake 72
Poached Pomegranate Spiced Pears 73
Coconut Rice Pudding 74

VEGETARIAN RICE COOKER MEALS COOKBOOK 75

BREAKFAST 76

Frittata with Summer Vegetables 77
Vanilla Almond Steel-Cut Oatmeal 78
Avocado Breakfast Bowl 79
Rice Cooker Oatmeal 80
Creamy Grits 81
Steel Cut Oats 82
Creamy Oatmeal 83
Tapioca Pudding 84

RICE DISHES 85

Dill and Lemon Rice with Feta 86
Spanish Rice 87
Fragrant Basmati Rice 88
Carrots and Peas Rice 89
Lemon Rice 90
Orange Chipotle Risotto 91
Moroccan Brown Rice 92
Rice Pilaf 93
Mexican Rice 94
Italian Rice and Peas 95

Caribbean Rice *96*
Mexican Green Rice *97*
Easy Coconut Rice *98*
Vegetable Rice Pilaf *99*
Quick and Easy Spinach Rice *100*
Chile Cheese Rice *101*
Toasted Coconut Yellow Rice *102*
Wild Berry Rice *103*
Brown Rice with Miso *104*
Saffron & Fruit Chutney Yellow Rice *105*
Sushi Rice *106*
Rice and Black Beans *107*
Easy Jambalaya Curry *108*
Polynesian Rice *109*
Quick and Easy Curry Rice *110*

NON-RICE DISHES 111

Rice Cooker Mac & Cheese *112*
Very Cheesy Polenta *113*
Steamed Tofu & Asparagus *114*
Southwest-Style Quinoa *115*
Kimchi *116*
Rice Cooker Quinoa *117*
Cheesy Paprika Mac 'n Cheese *118*
Pasta Cubano *119*
Quinoa Pomegranate salad *120*
Potato Salad *121*
Black Bean Chili *122*
Rice Cooker Polenta *123*
Rice Cooker Quinoa *124*
Jamaican Grits *125*

DESSERTS 126

Gingerbread Cake 127
Rice Pudding 128
Coconut-Pecan Upside Down Cake 129
Apple Rice Pudding 130
Chocolate Cake 131

THANK YOU 132

M<small>EASUREMENT</small> C<small>ONVERSIONS</small>

Liquid/Volume Measurements (approximate)

1 teaspoon = 1/6 fluid ounce (oz.) = 1/3 tablespoon = 5 ml

1 tablespoon = 1/2 fluid ounce (oz.) = 3 teaspoons = 15 ml

1 fluid ounce (oz.) = 2 tablespoons = 1/8 cup = 30 ml

1/4 cup = 2 fluid ounces (oz.) = 4 tablespoons = 60 ml

1/3 cup = 2⅔ fluid ounces (oz.) = 5 ⅓ tablespoons = 80 ml

1/2 cup = 4 fluid ounces (oz.) = 8 tablespoons = 120 ml

2/3 cup = 5⅓ fluid ounces (oz.) = 10⅔ tablespoons = 160 ml

3/4 cup = 6 fluid ounces (oz.) = 12 tablespoons = 180 ml

7/8 cup = 7 fluid ounces (oz.) = 14 tablespoons = 210 ml

1 cup = 8 fluid ounces (oz.) = 1/2 pint = 240 ml

1 pint = 16 fluid ounces (oz.) = 2 cups = 1/2 quart = 475 ml

1 quart = 4 cups = 32 fluid ounces (oz.) = 2 pints = 950 ml

1 liter = 1.055 quarts = 4.22 cups = 2.11 pints = 1000 ml

1 gallon = 4 quarts = 8 pints = 3.8 liters

Dry/Weight Measurements (approximate)

1 ounce (oz.) = 30 grams (g)

2 ounces (oz.) = 55 grams (g)

3 ounces (oz.) = 85 grams (g)

1/4 pound (lb.) = 4 ounces (oz.) = 125 grams (g)

1/2 pound (lb.) = 8 ounces (oz.) = 240 grams (g)

3/4 pound (lb.) = 12 ounces (oz.) = 375 grams (g)

1 pound (lb.) = 16 ounces (oz.) = 455 grams (g)

2 pounds (lbs.) = 32 ounces (oz.) = 910 grams (g)

1 kilogram (kg) = 2.2 pounds (lbs.) = 1000 gram (g)

INTRODUCTION

The rice cooker is the perfect home appliance for cooking, and is hands down the simplest way to make meals. No longer do you need to worry about burnt rice or having to keep an eye on a pot on the stove. Just pop in some rice and water, hit the cook button and let it go. Hot and soft rice every time all the time. Plus, prep and cleanup time is left to the absolute minimum.

More importantly, rice cookers are a time-saving replacement for traditional cooking and can be used for a lot more than just rice. This includes soups, cakes, oatmeal, frittatas, and so much more! Stop being dissatisfied with the same old recipes or looking up new ones that are just tedious and confusing, and prepare your taste buds for a splendidly delicious adventure! This cookbook contains over 60 delectable recipes for breakfast, main dishes, soups, and desserts that will surprise yourself and others. So plug in that rice cooker and let's start cooking!

*The following recipes can be used on simple rice cookers with only an on/off button to more advanced types. The rice cooker should be at least 4 cups capacity, and recipes should be adjust accordingly if smaller. Unless otherwise stated all ingredients should be measured using standard measuring cups instead of the rice cooker cup.

Quick & Easy

RICE COOKER MEALS

COOKBOOK

Over 60 recipes for breakfast, main dishes, soups, and desserts

By Susan Evans

BREAKFAST

Avocado Breakfast Bowl

SERVINGS: 2
PREP TIME: 10 min.
TOTAL TIME: 30 min.

Ingredients

- 1/2 cup water
- 1/4 cup red quinoa
- 1 1/2 teaspoons olive oil
- 2 eggs
- 1 pinch salt and ground black pepper to taste
- 1/4 teaspoon seasoned salt
- 1/4 teaspoon ground black pepper
- 1 avocado, diced
- 2 tablespoons crumbled feta cheese

Instructions

1. Combine water and quinoa together in a rice cooker. Cook until quinoa is tender, around 15 minutes.
2. Heat olive oil in a skillet over medium heat. Cook eggs as desired an; season with salt and pepper.
3. Combine quinoa and eggs in a bowl.
4. Top with avocado and feta cheese.

Rice Cooker Oatmeal

SERVINGS: 3
PREP TIME: 5 min.
TOTAL TIME: 30 min.

Ingredients

- 1 1/4 cups large flake rolled oats
- 2 tablespoons wheat bran
- 1 pinch salt
- 1/3 cup raisins or 1/3 cup fresh or dried fruit (optional)
- 2 1/2 cups water

Instructions

1. Put all ingredients in a rice cooker and turn on. It should be done around 25 to 30 minutes. Stir once during cooking.
2. Sprinkle with some ground flaxseed, sugar, and light cream; if desired.

Coconut Tapioca Pudding

SERVINGS: 6
PREP TIME: 10 min.
TOTAL TIME: 1 hour

Ingredients

- 3 1/4 cups canned unsweetened coconut milk
- 3/4 cup small pearl tapioca
- 3/4 cup sugar
- 1 large egg, beaten
- 1 pinch salt
- 2 1/2 teaspoons pure vanilla extract

Instructions

1. Combine and stir all ingredients except vanilla in bowl of 6-cup rice cooker (adjust amounts if smaller). Close cover and set for Porridge cycle or regular Cook setting.
2. Stir briefly every 20 minutes, and always reclose cover.
3. At end of cycle, remove bowl from cooker. Stir in vanilla and pour into a large serving bowl or serving dishes.
4. Serve warm, or refrigerate covered with plastic wrap.

Quick and Easy Oats

SERVINGS: 2
PREP TIME: 10 min.
TOTAL TIME: 20 min.

Ingredients

- 1 cup quick-cooking oats
- 1 cup water 1 cup milk
- 2 tablespoons honey
- 1 tablespoon white sugar
- 1 teaspoon vanilla extract
- 1 pinch salt

Instructions

1. Mix oats, water, milk, honey, sugar, vanilla extract, and salt in a rice cooker.
2. Cook oats in rice cooker until desired consistency, about 10 to 15 minutes.

Steel Cut Oatmeal

SERVINGS: 3
PREP TIME: 5 min.
TOTAL TIME: 15 min

Ingredients

- 3/4 cup steel cut oats
- 2 cups water
- 1/4 teaspoon salt
- 1/4 teaspoon pure vanilla extract
- 2 tablespoons raisins
- 1/2 cup of honey, if desired
- 1 teaspoon ground cinnamon, if desired
- Some dried fruit, if desired

Instructions

1. Place ingredients into the Rice cooker pot. Press cook. It should be done in 10-15 minutes.

Frittata in a Rice Cooker

SERVINGS: 4
PREP TIME: 15 min.
TOTAL TIME: 30 min.

Ingredients

- 1/2 cup frozen spinach, thawed, drained and squeezed dry
- 1/2 cup fresh button mushrooms, cleaned and sliced
- 2 green onions, chopped
- 4 large eggs, beaten
- 1/2 teaspoon ground oregano
- 1/2 teaspoon ground thyme
- 1 pinch salt & freshly ground black pepper
- 1/4 cup asiago cheese, grated

Instructions

1. Coat the rice cooker with non-stick cooking spray. In a medium bowl, combine and mix the spinach, mushrooms and onions. Add the eggs, oregano, thyme, salt, pepper and cheese. Combine and mix well.
2. Spoon frittata into the rice cooker. Close lid and press Cook until the eggs are firm on the bottom and almost set on the top, about 15 minutes. Use a spatula to slice the frittata into wedges.
3. Serve warm.

Tapioca Pudding

SERVINGS: 4
PREP TIME: 5 min.
TOTAL TIME: 25 min

Ingredients

- 3 tablespoons small pearl tapioca
- 2 cups milk
- 1 large egg
- 1/2 cup sugar
- 1 pinch salt
- 1 teaspoon pure vanilla extract

Instructions

1. Place tapioca in rice cooker. In a small bowl, whisk together milk, egg, sugar, and salt. Pour milk mix over the tapioca and stir to combine. Cover and set to Porridge cycle or to Cook for 20 minutes.
2. When it switches to Warm cycle, remove bowl from cooker and stir in vanilla. Pour pudding into a large bowl or individual dishes.
3. Let cool.
4. Serve warm, if desired, or refrigerate covered with plastic wrap.

CHICKEN RICE DISHES

Spinach, Mushroom, and Chicken Risotto

SERVINGS: 4
PREP TIME: 5 min.
TOTAL TIME: 25 min.

Ingredients

- 1 tablespoon extra-virgin olive oil
- Salt and pepper, to taste
- 1 lb skinless chicken breast, cut into 1-inch pieces
- 4 cups spinach, washed and dried thoroughly
- 3 cups chicken broth
- 1/4 cup grated parmesan cheese
- 1 cup superfine Arborio medium grain rice
- 1 lb mushroom, crimini, sautéed

Instructions

1. Add spinach, rice, and liquid to rice cooker bowl and press Cook button.
2. Heat olive oil in a sauté pan. Sauté chicken on all sides, until no longer pink in the center. Remove pan from heat and set aside.
3. When cooker switches to Warm, mix in chicken, mushrooms and cheese. Replace lid and let rice steam for another 5 minutes the Warm setting.
4. Season to taste with kosher salt and freshly ground black pepper.

Garlic Chicken Fragrant Rice

SERVINGS: 5
PREP TIME: 10 min.
TOTAL TIME: 35 min.

Ingredients

- 3 cups uncooked jasmine rice
- 3 cups water
- 2 tablespoons sesame oil
- 2 cubes chicken bouillon
- 1/2 cup olive oil
- 1 green onion, chopped
- 2 cloves garlic, smashed
- 1 (2 inch) piece fresh ginger root, crushed
- 1 chicken thigh with skin

Instructions

1. Place rice, water, sesame oil, chicken bouillon, olive oil, green onion, garlic and ginger in a rice cooker. Stir, and place chicken thigh on top. Turn on rice cooker.
2. Serve warm.

Oriental Chicken and Rice

SERVINGS: 6
PREP/ TOTAL TIME: 30 min

Ingredients

- 1 bell pepper, chopped
- 1 onion, top chopped
- 1 1/2 cups rice
- 1 (14 ounce) can chicken broth or 1 chicken bouillon cube
- 1 (8 ounce) can water chestnuts
- 1 (6 ounce) can chicken
- 1 (8 ounce) can sliced mushrooms
- 1/2 cup butter

Instructions

1. Mix ingredients in rice cooker. Set button to Cook. When cooker goes off dish is done.
2. Serve with rice.

Yellow Chicken Flavored Rice

SERVINGS: 10
PREP TIME: 10 min.
TOTAL TIME: 30 min.

Ingredients

- 4 cups chicken stock
- 3 cups long-grain white rice
- 3 tablespoons tomato sauce
- 2 tablespoons olive oil
- 2 tablespoons salt
- 2 packages (1.41 ounce) sazon seasoning with annatto
- 1 tablespoon garlic powder
- 1 cube chicken bouillon, crushed

Instructions

1. Place chicken stock, rice, tomato sauce, olive oil, salt, sazon seasoning, garlic powder, and chicken bouillon in the rice cooker. Stir to combine. Cover and cook for one cycle until rice is tender and fluffy.
2. Serve warm.

Curry Chicken Jambalaya

SERVINGS: 4
PREP TIME: 5 min.
TOTAL TIME: 30 min.

Ingredients

- 2 tablespoons oil
- 1 cup chopped onion
- 1 tablespoon minced garlic
- 2 tablespoons curry powder
- 2 cups water
- 1 (8 ounce) can tomato sauce
- 1 (8 ounce) package jambalaya mix
- 1 lb. boneless skinless chicken breast, cut into 1-inch cubes
- 1/2 cup golden raisin
- 3/4 cup plain yogurt
- 1/3 cup chopped cashews

Instructions

1. Place oil in a rice cooker, and add onion and garlic. Push cook button and stir 5 minutes or until onion is tender. Add curry powder. Push cook button and stir 2 minutes.
2. Mix in water, tomato sauce, Jambalaya Mix chicken and raisins. Push cook button and cover with lid. After cooker switches to Warm, turn off and stir in yogurt.
3. Let stand for 5 minutes. Sprinkle with cashews.

Sesame Chicken Rice

SERVINGS: 6
PREP TIME: 10 min.
TOTAL TIME: 35 min.

Ingredients

- 2 tablespoons peanut oil
- 1 teaspoon sesame oil
- 1 tablespoon finely grated fresh ginger
- 2 garlic cloves, peeled and crushed
- 2 onions, peeled and finely sliced
- 450 ml short-grain rice
- 2 cups chopped cooked chicken
- 1/4 cup chopped shallot
- 2 tablespoons toasted sesame seeds
- 3 cups chicken stock

Instructions

1. Place peanut and sesame oils into cooking bowl and press Cook. Heat for 1 minute.
2. Stir in ginger, garlic and onions. Cook for 2 minutes Add washed rice, cook for 1 min, constantly stirring.
3. Pour in chicken stock and cook, covered until rice cooker switches to Warm. Gently mix chicken, shallots and sesame seeds.
4. Replace lid and stand for 10 mins on the Warm mode before serving.

Ginger Chicken and Rice

SERVINGS: 4
PREP/TOTAL TIME: 45 min.

Ingredients

- 1 large chicken bouillon cube
- 3/4 cup hot water
- 1 cup jasmine rice
- 1 1/4 pounds skinless, boneless chicken thighs, cut into 1-inch cubes
- 1 2-inch piece of fresh ginger, peeled and cut into matchsticks
- 3 packed cups baby spinach
- 1 cup unsweetened coconut milk
- Kosher salt

Instructions

1. Dissolve the bouillon cube in the hot water in a small bowl.
2. Combine the rice with the chicken and ginger in a rice cooker. Arrange the spinach on top. Pour the coconut milk and bouillon broth and lightly season with salt. Turn the cooker on to Cook. After it goes off, let stand for 5 minutes.
3. Fluff rice with a fork, spoon into bowls and serve.

Rice, Artichoke, Spinach, and Chicken Salad

SERVINGS: 8
PREP TIME: 25 min.
TOTAL TIME: 1 hour 5 min

Ingredients

- 2 tablespoons olive oil
- 1 cup diced onion
- 2 cloves garlic, minced
- 1/2 cup pine nuts
- 1 lemon, zested
- 1 teaspoon vegetable bouillon
- 1/2 teaspoon ground turmeric
- 2 cups rice
- 4 cups water
- 1 bunch green onions
- 1/4 cup torn fresh basil leaves
- 10 small thinly sliced fresh mushrooms
- 1 bunch fresh spinach, roughly chopped
- 2 cups diced cooked chicken breast
- 1 cup roughly chopped marinated artichoke hearts
- 1 cup shredded Parmesan cheese
- ground black pepper to taste

Instructions

1. Heat oil in a pot over medium-high heat. Sauté onion and garlic in hot oil until onion has softened, 5 to 7 minutes. Stir pine nuts into onion mix. Sauté until fragrant and golden, about 2 to 3 minutes. Stir in lemon zest, vegetable bouillon, and turmeric into onion mixture. Sauté until fragrant, for about 1 minute. Add rice to mixture and cook until fragrant, 2 to 3 more minutes.
2. Pour rice mix in a rice cooker and add water. Set rice cooker to Cook and select Start. Fluff cooked rice with a fork and top with green onion and basil. Cover rice cooker and steam green onion and basil until tender, about 5 minutes.

3. Stir mushrooms into rice and place spinach on top. Cover rice cooker again and steam until spinach is slightly wilted, about 5 minutes. Add chicken, artichoke hearts, and Parmesan cheese. Stir to combine.
4. Season with black pepper.

SEAFOOD RICE DISHES

Cajun Crawfish Tails with Rice

SERVINGS: 6
PREP TIME: 15 min.
TOTAL TIME: 45 min.

Ingredients

- 1 1/2 cups uncooked long grain rice
- 1 green bell pepper, diced
- 1 small onion, diced
- 1 bunch green onions, diced
- 1 lb peeled crawfish tails
- 1 (14.5 ounce) can chicken broth
- 1 (10 ounce) can diced tomatoes with green chile peppers
- 4 tablespoons margarine
- 1 tablespoon dried parsley
- 1 teaspoon Cajun seasoning, or to taste

Instructions

1. Combine rice, green pepper, onion, green onions, crawfish tails, chicken broth, diced tomatoes, margarine, parsley, and Cajun seasoning in a large bowl.
2. Pour into rice cooker, and cook for one cycle, or until liquid is absorbed (about 30 minutes).
3. Adjust seasonings to taste. Serve warm.

Shrimp Jambalaya

SERVINGS: 6
PREP TIME: 15 min.
TOTAL TIME: 1 hour 15 min

Ingredients

- 2 cups rice
- 1 pound shrimp, or more to taste, peeled and deveined
- 1 can (14.5 ounce) chicken broth
- 1 can (10 ounce) tomato sauce, or to taste
- 1 bell pepper, minced
- 1/2 cup margarine
- 1 jar (4 ounce) mushrooms, undrained

Instructions

1. Rinse rice and drain.
2. Mix rinsed rice, shrimp, chicken broth, tomato sauce, bell pepper, margarine, and mushrooms in a rice cooker.
3. Press Start and let cook until the liquid is bubbling around 10 to 15 minutes. Stir once, replace cover, and continue until the end of the cycle.
4. Serve warm.

Salmon Risotto with Rice

SERVINGS: 4
PREP TIME: 5 min.
TOTAL TIME: 25 min.

Ingredients

- 1 onion, chopped finely
- 2 garlic cloves, minced
- 1 2/3 cups Arborio rice
- 200 ml dry white wine
- 2 tablespoons lemon juice
- 500 ml chicken stock
- 2 tablespoons shredded parmesan cheese
- 1 shallot (green part)
- 1 tablespoon capers
- 2 teaspoons dill
- 1 tablespoon balsamic vinegar
- 200 grams fresh salmon, skin off and deboned
- salt and pepper
- dill, extra, to serve

Instructions

1. Stir and combine garlic, onion, rice, white wine, lemon juice and chicken stock in the rice cooker. Hit cook button. About 3/4 of the way through cooking of the rice, open the rice cooker and stir.
2. Cover salmon with balsamic and marinate in a separate dish. Put steamer rack on top of the rice and put the salmon in the steamer. (If rice cooker doesn't have a steamer, cook the salmon for a few minutes in the microwave). Once rice cooker stops cooking, leave it on Warm setting. Open the rice cooker, take out the salmon, add the cheese, stir rice, and cover rice cooker again.
3. Flake salmon into small chunks and cut the shallot into small slices. Open rice cooker, add flaked salmon, shallot, capers and dill. Mix well and season with salt and pepper to taste. Cover the rice cooker.
4. Serve, and sprinkle with extra dill.

Seafood Jambalaya

SERVINGS: 8
PREP TIME: 5 min.
TOTAL TIME: 35 min.

Ingredients

- 1 lb raw shrimp
- 1 (6 ounce) jar oysters or 1 lb crabmeat
- 1 1/2 cups raw rice
- 1/2-1 cup melted butter or melted margarine
- 1 medium onion, chopped
- 1 medium bell pepper, chopped
- 1/2 cup onion tops, chopped
- 1 teaspoon chopped garlic
- 1 (10 1/2 ounce) can beef broth
- 1 (4 ounce) can mushrooms, drained
- seasoning

Instructions

1. Mix everything in rice cooker. Season to taste.
2. Press cook on rice cooker.
3. Serve warm.

Easy Rice-Cooker Shrimp Jambalaya

SERVINGS: 6
PREP TIME: 15 min.
TOTAL TIME: 45 min.

Ingredients

- 1 cup mushroom pieces, optional
- 1 teaspoon minced garlic clove
- 1/2 small onion, diced
- 1/2 green bell pepper, cut into chunks
- 3 cups chicken broth
- 1/2 lb shrimp
- 2 teaspoons butter or 2 teaspoons margarine
- 1 1/2 cups white rice
- 1 (15 ounce) can diced tomatoes
- 1 cayenne pepper, to taste

Instructions

1. Sauté garlic, onion, bell pepper, and mushrooms if using, in butter or margarine in a medium frying pan over medium heat, for 5-10 minutes or until the onions are translucent.
2. Add and stir in rice, shrimp, vegetables, chicken broth, diced tomatoes, and cayenne pepper in rice cooker. Set rice cooker to cook and let sit 10 minutes after it has finished.
3. Stir and serve.

RED MEAT RICE DISHES

Bacon Fried Rice

SERVINGS: 4
PREP TIME: 10 min.
TOTAL TIME: 30 min.

Ingredients

- 2 cups rice
- 2 cups beef stock
- 1 tablespoon oil
- 250 g bacon, cut into strips
- 1 onion, sliced
- 1 teaspoon minced garlic
- 1 cup frozen mixed vegetables, corn kernels and peas will do
- 2 tablespoons soy sauce

Instructions

1. Add oil, bacon, onion and garlic to rice cooker and press start. Stir frequently until onion has softened. Add rice and coat in oil.
2. Add frozen vegetable and beef stock and combine well. Place lid on and cook.
3. When it is done cooking, mix in soy sauce.
4. Stir and serve.

Jambalaya Sausage with Beans

SERVINGS: 5
PREP TIME: 5 min.
TOTAL TIME: 40 min

Ingredients

- 1/2 lb. smoked sausage, thinly sliced
- 1/2 can (about a 1/2 cup) French onion soup
- 1/2 cup water
- 1 can Rotel or diced tomatoes, undrained
- 1 can black-eyed peas, undrained
- 2 cups uncooked rice

Instructions

1. Mix all ingredients in rice cooker and press Cook. When done allow to stand for 5 minutes and keep covered.
2. Turn rice cooker back on. This will cook for a shorter cycle. Let it stand for 10 minutes after it goes off.
3. Stir and check rice to make sure it is done. If not, add about 2 tablespoon more water, stir, and set it to cook again.
4. Serve.

Chinese Sausage and Rice

SERVINGS: 6
PREP TIME: 5 min.
TOTAL TIME: 1 hour

Ingredients

- 2 cups medium grain white rice
- 1 cup Chinese sausage, thinly sliced on the diagonal
- 1/2 cup green onion, thinly sliced
- 2 3/4 cups water
- 1/4 cup cilantro leaf, for garnish
- 2 tablespoons black sesame seeds, for garnish

Instructions

1. Rinse the rice in a strainer. Add the drained rice, sausage, and onions to the rice bowl. Add water and stir to combine.
2. Cook on the regular setting. When it switches to Warm let steam for 15 minutes. Fluff the rice with a wooden spoon.
3. Place in a serving dish, and garnish with the cilantro and the sesame seeds.

Jambalaya with Sausage

SERVINGS: 6
PREP TIME: 20 min.
TOTAL TIME: 45 min.

Ingredients

- 1/2 cup peanut oil
- 1 large onion, chopped
- 1 1/2 lbs smoked sausage, sliced
- 1 bell pepper, chopped
- 2 cloves garlic, chopped
- 3 bay leaves
- 1/4 teaspoon thyme
- 1 teaspoon black pepper
- 1 package frozen mixed vegetables
- 1 cup mild salsa or 1 cup canned tomato (optional)
- 3 cups rice, uncooked
- water

Instructions

1. Heat oil in large frying pan. Sauté onions, sausage, and bell pepper. Cook until onion and pepper is tender and sausage is cooked.
2. Add chopped tomato and garlic to pan and sauté until cooked.
3. Place 3 cups of rice in rice cooker and enough water to reach the Paella or Sweet rice level marked on rice cooker. Place sausage and vegetables, package of frozen vegetables, bay leaves, thyme, parsley, black pepper, and salsa if desired. Press the cooking button.

Bacon and Onion Rice

SERVINGS: 4
PREP/TOTAL TIME: 20 min.

Ingredients

- 1 1/2 cups uncooked white rice
- 3 tablespoons butter or 3 tablespoons margarine
- 4 -6 slices bacon
- 1/2 medium onion

Instructions

1. Cut onion into 1/2 inch chunks and slice bacon into small 1/4 inch square pieces. Place rice in rice cooker and add water as recommended (usually 2 cups). Set rice-cooker to Cook.
2. Heat medium-sized frying pan over medium heat. Fry bacon and onion until bacon is crisp.
3. When rice is finished, add in butter or margarine. Stir to combine.
4. Add and stir in bacon and onion mixture.

Rice-Cooker Jambalaya

SERVINGS: 6
PREP TIME: 15 min.
TOTAL TIME: 45 min.

Ingredients

- 1 cup mushroom pieces, optional
- 1 teaspoon minced garlic clove
- 1/2 small onion, diced
- 1/2 green bell pepper, cut into chunks
- 3 cups chicken broth
- 1/2 lb kielbasa, cut into small pieces
- 2 teaspoons butter or 2 teaspoons margarine
- 1 1/2 cups white rice
- 1 (15 ounce) can diced tomatoes
- 1 cayenne pepper, to taste

Instructions

1. Sauté garlic, onion, bell pepper, and mushrooms if using, in butter or margarine in a medium frying pan over medium heat, for 5-10 minutes or until the onions are translucent. Add sausage and cook another 1-2 minutes.
2. Add and stir in rice, sausage, vegetables, chicken broth, diced tomatoes, and cayenne pepper in rice cooker. Set rice cooker to cook and let sit 10 minutes after it has finished.
3. Stir and serve.

OTHER RICE DISHES

Mexican Rice

SERVINGS: 6
PREP/TOTAL TIME: 25 min.

Ingredients

- 1 cup rice
- 2 1/4 cups low sodium chicken broth
- 6 ounce tomato paste
- 2 tablespoons butter
- 1/2 cup onion, diced
- 1 garlic clove, small, minced
- 4 ounces diced green chilies
- 1 dash pepper
- 1 dash red pepper flakes
- cilantro or parsley

Instructions

1. Combine and stir in ingredients in rice cooker. Press cook.
2. When cooking is finished let stand uncovered for 3 minutes.
3. Stir before serving.

Dill and Lemon Rice with Feta

SERVINGS: 3
PREP TIME: 5 min.
TOTAL TIME: 45 min.

Ingredients

- 1 1/2 cups long grain white rice
- 2 cups chicken stock
- 2 tablespoons olive oil
- 2 small boiling onions, chopped
- 1/4 cup pine nuts
- 1/4 cup fresh lemon juice
- 1 tablespoon minced fresh dill
- 1 1/2 teaspoons minced of fresh mint, optional
- 1 cup crumbled feta
- 1 lemon, cut in 8 wedges

Instructions

1. Coat rice bowl with cooking spray. Add rice and stock. Set for the regular white rice or Cook cycle.
2. When it switches to Warm, let stand and steam for 10 minutes.
3. Heat olive oil in a small skillet. Add onions and cook for 5 minutes, frequently stirring until soft. Add pine nuts. Cook and stir until golden, about a minute.
4. Add the onion and pine nut mixture to the rice, along with the lemon juice, dill, and mint (if using). Stir with a plastic rice paddle or a wooden spoon to combine.
5. Cover and continue on Warm setting for 10 more minutes.
6. Transfer to a serving dish, and top with the feta and lemon wedges.

Cajun Wild Rice

SERVINGS: 6
PREP TIME: 10 min.
TOTAL TIME: 55 min.

Ingredients

- 1 cup uncooked wild rice
- 1 (14 ounce) can chicken broth
- 1/4 cup water
- 1/2 pound andouille sausage, diced
- 1/2 cup diced sweet onion
- 1 cup chopped fresh mushrooms
- 1 tablespoon minced garlic
- 1 (10.75 ounce) can condensed cream of mushroom soup

Instructions

1. Combine wild rice, chicken broth, water, sausage, onion, mushrooms and garlic in rice cooker. Press button to cook. Bring to a boil, then reduce heat to low, cover, and simmer for 25 to 30 minutes, or until rice is tender.
2. Let stand and stir in the cream of mushroom soup.

Chile Cheese Rice

SERVINGS: 8
PREP TIME: 10 min.
TOTAL TIME: 25 min.

Ingredients

- 2 cups white rice, using rice cooker cups
- 3 cups chicken broth or 3 cups water or 3 cups vegetable broth
- 1 (4 ounce) can diced green chilies
- 1/2 medium onion, diced
- 2 teaspoons garlic
- 1 cup Monterey jack cheese, shredded
- 1 tablespoon margarine

Instructions

1. Sauté onion and garlic in margarine in a small saucepan over medium heat, until onion becomes translucent.
2. Place rice, sautéed onion and garlic, chilies, and chicken broth in rice cooker. Stir to combine. Set cooker to Cook setting. When cooked, mix in shredded cheese and let sit 5-10 minutes.

Caribbean Rice

SERVINGS: 4
PREP TIME: 15 min.
TOTAL TIME: 40 min.

Ingredients

- 1 cup white rice, rinsed
- 1 teaspoon ground Jamaican jerk spice or seasoning
- 1/4 cup cilantro or 1/4 cup parsley
- 1 sprig thyme, stem discarded
- 1 garlic clove, minced
- 1 teaspoon grated fresh ginger
- 2 scallions, sliced
- 3/4 cup finely diced sweet potato
- 1/3 cup toasted coconut
- 1/3 cup raisins
- 1/3 cup diced red pepper
- 1 cup vegetable broth, to cover rice

Instructions

1. Place all the ingredients in rice cooker, except for 1 tablespoon scallions and 1 teaspoon coconut which should be saved for garnish. Pour broth 3/4 inch above the level of the rice. Press the cook button.
2. When cooked, fluff with fork. Place in a serving dish and top with reserved coconut and scallions. Place lime alongside for garnish.

Rice and Lentils

SERVINGS: 6
PREP TIME: 5 min.
TOTAL TIME: 35 min.

Ingredients

- 2 cups white rice
- 1 cup brown lentils
- 1 cup pearled barley
- 1/4 cup olive oil
- 2 tablespoons minced garlic
- 2 tablespoons chicken stock concentrate
- water as needed

Instructions

1. Rinse rice, lentils, and barley thoroughly. Mix in a rice cooker and add olive oil, garlic, and stock concentrate. Stir.
2. Pour enough water to reach the 4 1/2-cup mark on the rice cooker.
3. Press Start and cook until the rice and lentils are tender.

Easy Risotto

SERVINGS: 6
PREP TIME: 5 min.
TOTAL TIME: 45 min.

Ingredients

- 1 1/2 cups Arborio rice
- 4 1/2 cups hot chicken stock
- 1 cup grated Parmesan cheese (optional)

Instructions

1. Place rice and heated chicken stock into rice cooker.
2. Press Start and let cook until the cycle is completed and shifts to Warm setting. Let rice stand with cover on until rice is tender, about 10 minutes.
3. Sprinkle Parmesan cheese over the rice. Stir and serve.

Saffron & Fruit Chutney Yellow Rice

SERVINGS: 6
PREP/TOTAL TIME: 5 min.
TOTAL TIME: 35 min.

Ingredients

- 3 cups basmati rice, rinsed
- 3 cups water, to the rice cooker level
- 1 pinch powdered saffron (about 5 - 8 strands) or 1 pinch saffron strand (about 5 - 8 strands)
- 2 tablespoons fruit chutney
- 2 -4 cardamom pods, split & use seeds
- salt and pepper
- 1 ounce butter
- 2 -4 sprigs fresh coriander, optional

Instructions

1. Place 3 cups of rinsed Basmati rice in rice cooker, using cup provided. Fill up with water to the 3 cup level. Add saffron, cardamom seeds, salt, pepper & chutney to the rice and water. Using the special non-stick spatula, gently mix. Turn on to the Cook cycle.
2. When ready to serve, add the butter and gently combine. Garnish with chopped fresh coriander/cilantro. Top with some toasted flaked almonds.

Rice and Black Beans

SERVINGS: 4
PREP TIME: 5 min.
TOTAL TIME: 35 min.

Ingredients

- 1 cup uncooked rice
- 1 can (10 ounce) diced tomatoes with green chilies (Rotel)
- 1 can (14 1/2 ounce) chicken broth
- 1 can (15 1/4 ounce) black beans
- 1 can (14 3/4 ounce) sweet corn (optional)
- 1 cup cheese (optional)

Instructions

1. Drain tomatoes, black beans, and corn. Place in Rice Cooker. Add rice, chicken broth and stir. Cook until cooker stops.
2. Top with cheese and serve.

NON-RICE DISHES

Curried Squash and Pork

SERVINGS: 6
PREP TIME: 20 min.
TOTAL TIME: 1 hour

Ingredients

- 1 tablespoon peanut oil
- 7/8 lb boneless sirloin pork chop, diced
- 1 1/2 tablespoons curry powder
- 2 carrots, sliced
- 1/2 onion, chopped
- 1 teaspoon fresh minced garlic (optional)
- 13 ounce low-fat coconut milk
- 14 ounce can chicken broth, undiluted
- 1/4 cup water
- 19 ounce can chickpeas, drained and rinsed
- 3/4 cup uncooked brown rice
- 1 cup raw acorn squash, diced

Instructions

1. Brown meat in hot oil on steam setting (must close for meat to brown). Add vegetables and cook for 5 minutes. If there is no steam setting, cook in a skillet.
2. Combine all the ingredients in rice cooker and press Cook.

Very Cheesy Polenta

SERVINGS: 4
PREP TIME: 10 min.
TOTAL TIME: 40 min.

Ingredients

- 2 tablespoons butter
- 1/2 onion, chopped
- 1 clove garlic, minced
- 1 cup chicken broth
- 1 cup milk
- 1/2 cup polenta
- 1/4 teaspoon salt, or more to taste
- 2 ounces shredded Cheddar cheese
- 2 ounces shredded Parmesan cheese
- 1/4 teaspoon freshly ground black pepper

Instructions

1. Place butter, onion, and garlic in rice cooker. Cover and set cooker on. Cook until onion is soft and translucent, about 10 to 15 minutes, stirring occasionally.
2. Add chicken broth, milk, polenta, and salt. Cover and cook on full cycle, occasionally stirring until polenta absorbs the liquid, around 20 minutes.
3. Add Cheddar cheese, Parmesan cheese, and black pepper. Stir until cheese is melted.

Paprika Chicken

SERVINGS: 6
PREP TIME: 15 min.
TOTAL TIME: 55 min

Ingredients

- 3 tablespoons all-purpose flour
- 2 lbs. chicken breasts, cut into 1/2-inch strips
- 2 cups chopped onions (about 1 large)
- 1 1/4 cups chicken broth
- 2 tablespoons sweet Hungarian paprika
- 2 teaspoons minced garlic
- 1 teaspoon salt
- 1 teaspoon fresh ground black pepper
- 1 (8 ounce) package pre-sliced mushrooms
- 1 1/4 cups sour cream

Instructions

1. Place onions in cooker. Hit cook to brown onions.
2. In a medium bowl combine flour and chicken. Toss well. Add chicken mixture to chopped onion, until lightly browned. Add next 6 ingredients (except sour cream) into the pan. Hit cook.
3. When it switches to Warm, add sour cream and mix well. Allow to heat for a few minutes.
4. Serve it with noodles, rice or dumplings.

Pasta Cubano

SERVINGS: 3
PREP TIME: 15 min.
TOTAL TIME: 25 min

Ingredients

- 1 tablespoon olive oil
- 400 grams ground round
- 1 cup minced red or green bell peppers
- 1/2 cup minced onions salt, to taste
- 1 teaspoon ground cumin
- 1 teaspoon dried oregano
- 2 tablespoons Worcestershire sauce
- 2 cups water
- 1 cup canned diced tomatoes
- 2 tablespoons sliced green olives
- 1 teaspoon olive oil
- 2 cups uncooked elbow macaroni or penne
- grated Parmesan cheese, for topping

Instructions

1. Heat olive oil in a medium pan. Add ground round and cook until browned. Add and sauté bell peppers and minced onions, until fragrant and soft. Season with salt, cumin, and oregano. Remove from heat. Add Worcestershire sauce.
2. Transfer beef mixture to the rice cooker. Add and mix in water, diced tomatoes, olives, olive oil, and uncooked pasta. Turn on the rice cooker.
3. Check the pasta when it switches to the warm setting. If pasta is not yet cooked, add more water and turn the rice cooker on again.
4. To avoid the pasta becoming soft, do not leave the rice cooker on warm for a long time.
5. Once pasta is al dente, transfer to serving plate and top with cheese.

Potato Salad

SERVINGS: 6
PREP TIME: 10 min.
TOTAL TIME: 30 min. + refrigeration

Ingredients

- 1 1/2 lbs small potatoes
- 1 1/2 cups water, for rice cooker
- 1 1/2 cups mayonnaise
- 1 tablespoon extra-virgin olive oil
- 1 -2 tablespoon vinegar
- 1 teaspoon celery seed
- 2 tablespoons chopped onions
- 1 -2 stalk celery, chopped
- 2 teaspoons prepared mustard
- 1 -2 tablespoon pickle relish
- 1/2 teaspoon salt, to taste
- 2 -4 hard-boiled eggs, coarsely chopped
- Paprika, for garnish

Instructions

1. Cut potatoes into bite size pieces and place in rice cooker with water. Turn rice cooker on and cook for 10-15 minutes, or until potatoes are done.
2. Place rice cooker pan in sink and run cold water in the pan to cool potatoes and eggs. Drain well.
3. Put potatoes in a bowl or container and add the rest of the ingredients. Combine well and refrigerate.

Roasted Pork

SERVINGS: 4
PREP TIME: 5 min.
TOTAL TIME: 50 min

Ingredients

- Any cut of pork, up to 2 lbs
- A bunch of scallions
- A thumb size ginger root, sliced
- 6 garlic cloves
- Salt and pepper
- 1 tablespoon oil
- 1 cup soy sauce
- 1 cup sugar
- 1 cup hoisin sauce

Instructions

1. Generously rub salt and pepper on the pork, and tie with kitchen twine if you wish.
2. Heat and fry garlic in a pan. Add the pork and caramelize the surface. (The pork doesn't need to be cooked through). If garlic begins to burn remove from the pan. Transfer pork to the rice cooker fat side down. Add fried garlic cloves, scallions, ginger, soy sauce, sugar and hoisin sauce.
3. To avoid overflowing do not fill liquid ingredients over than the top of liquid lines in the rice cooker. Turn on the rice cooker to cook. During the middle of cooking, open the rice cooker and turn the pork upside down to evenly cook. Go through another cooking cycle if the pork is not cooked throughout after the first cycle.
4. Take out the pork from the rice cooker and let cool. Cut into pieces for serving
5. Reserve the cooking liquid perhaps for a noodle soup.

Soy Chicken

SERVINGS: 4
PREP TIME: 10 min.
TOTAL TIME: 55 min. + refrigeration

Ingredients

- 1/2 cup soy sauce
- 6 cloves garlic, smashed
- 4 slices fresh ginger root, coarsely chopped
- 1 teaspoon monosodium glutamate (optional)
- 1 teaspoon salt
- 1/2 teaspoon ground black pepper
- 1/2 teaspoon sesame seed oil
- 4 boneless chicken thighs
- 1 1/2 teaspoons corn-starch
- 1 cup water, or as needed

Instructions

1. Place soy sauce, garlic, ginger, monosodium glutamate (if using), salt, pepper, and sesame oil into a large resealable plastic bag. Squeeze bag to mix the ingredients and dissolve the salt. Add chicken thighs to marinade and squeeze bag again to coat the chicken. Squeeze air out and zip the bag closed. Refrigerate for 1 hour.
2. In a small bowl, mix the corn-starch and 2 tablespoons of water until smooth. Pour marinade from plastic bag into the rice cooker. Mix in the corn-starch mixture until combined. Place chicken thighs into the sauce and add enough water to barely cover the chicken. Stir.
3. Close the lid of the cooker and press the Cook button. When steam begins to come out of the top of the cooker (after about 20 minutes), set timer for 10 minutes. When the timer goes off, uncover and stir the chicken. Set timer and cook for another 10 minutes. Switch cooker to Warm setting and leave for 20 minutes before serving.

Quinoa Pomegranate salad

SERVINGS: 4
PREP/ TOTAL TIME: 35 min.

Ingredients

- 2 cups quinoa, rinsed
- 4 cups water pinch of salt
- 1 cup pomegranate seeds
- 1/2 teaspoon all spice powder
- 1/2 cup chopped fresh mint
- 1 tablespoon pine nuts, toasted
- squeeze of lemon juice
- 1 teaspoon olive oil
- salt and cracked black pepper, to taste

Instructions

1. Place quinoa, water and a pinch of salt in the rice cooker. Turn it on.
2. Toast pine nuts while you wait.
3. When quinoa is done, combine all spice and lemon juice. Let it cool.
4. Add all other ingredients and combine.

Super Cheesy Polenta

SERVINGS: 4
PREP TIME: 10 min.
TOTAL TIME: 40 min.

Ingredients

- 2 tablespoons butter
- 1/2 onion, chopped
- 1 clove garlic, minced
- 1 cup chicken broth
- 1 cup milk
- 1/2 cup polenta
- 1/4 teaspoon salt, or more to taste
- 2 ounces shredded Cheddar cheese
- 2 ounces shredded Parmesan cheese
- 1/4 teaspoon freshly ground black pepper

Instructions

1. Place butter, onion, and garlic in rice cooker. Turn on cooker and close lid. Cook until onion is translucent and soft, occasionally stirring, 10 to 15 minutes.
2. Add chicken broth, milk, polenta, and salt. Cover and cook on full cycle, occasionally stirring, until liquid is absorbed, about 20 minutes.
3. Add Cheddar cheese, Parmesan cheese, and black pepper. Stir until cheese is melted.

Steamed Tofu & Asparagus

SERVINGS: 4
PREP TIME: 15 min.
TOTAL TIME: 35 min.

Ingredients

- 1/2 small asparagus bunch, 1 1/2-inch lengths
- 1/2 (6 oz.) fried tofu, cubed
- 1/2 small carrot, peeled, thinly sliced
- 1 clove garlic, minced
- 2 tablespoon oyster sauce *omit oyster sauce for vegetarian
- 1 tablespoon Aloha Shoyu
- 1 teaspoon vegetable oil
- 1 teaspoon sesame seed oil
- 1 teaspoon mirin
- 1 teaspoon honey

Instructions

1. Toss and combine all ingredients in rice cooker. Turn on rice cooker to cook.

Creamy Macaroni and Cheese

SERVINGS: 4
PREP/ TOTAL TIME: 20 min.

Ingredients

- 2 cups macaroni
- 1 cup chicken stock or 1 cup water
- 1 cup heavy cream or 1 cup half-and-half
- 1 1/2 cups shredded mixed cheeses (mild cheddar, Vermont cheddar, mozzarella, and fontina)
- 2 tablespoons butter
- 1/2 teaspoon salt and pepper
- 1 pinch cayenne pepper

Instructions

1. Place pasta and liquids into rice cooker. Close lid and press Cook.
2. When rice cooker goes to Warm, add other ingredients and stir. Close lid and keep warm until ready to serve.

Chicken Quinoa with Sun-dried Tomatoes

SERVINGS: 1
PREP TIME: 15 min.
TOTAL TIME: 1 hour

Ingredients

- 1 (6 ounce) chicken breast, cut into 1/2-inch cubes
- 3/4 cup water
- 3/8 cup white quinoa
- 1/4 cup chopped onion
- 1/4 cup sun-dried tomatoes, cut into strips
- 2 cloves garlic, minced
- 1/2 teaspoon curry powder
- ground black pepper to taste

Instructions

1. Combine chicken breast cubes, water, quinoa, onion, sun-dried tomatoes, garlic, curry powder, and ground black pepper in rice cooker. Press button to Cook.
2. Serve warm.

Cheesy Mac and Cheese

SERVINGS: 3
PREP TIME/TOTAL TIME: 30 min.

Ingredients

- 1 1/2 cups elbow macaroni
- 1 1/2 cups chicken broth or 1 1/2 cups water and a good-quality chicken bouillon cubes
- 1 cup heavy cream
- 3/4 cup shredded cheddar cheese
- 1/2 cup shredded mozzarella cheese
- 1/4 cup shredded parmesan cheese
- 1/4 teaspoon kosher salt, to taste
- 1/2 teaspoon dry mustard
- 1/2 teaspoon paprika
- 1/4 teaspoon pepper

Instructions

1. Combine macaroni, broth and cream in rice cooker. Press cook and stir occasionally. When machine switches to Warm, add remaining ingredients. Stir thoroughly until all cheese is melted. Press Cook again. After a few minutes it will switch to Warm.
2. Serve.

Rice Cooker Quinoa

SERVINGS: 4
PREP TIME: 2 min.
TOTAL TIME: 20 min.

Ingredients

- 1 cup quinoa
- 2 cups liquid (low-sodium chicken broth, low-sodium vegetable broth, or water)
- 1/2 teaspoon salt

Instructions

1. Rinse 1 cup of quinoa in cold water. Pour rinsed quinoa into rice cooker.
2. Add liquid and salt. Turn on your rice cooker.
3. Allow quinoa to set for 3 to 5 minutes. Fluff with a fork and serve.

Healthy Rice-Cooker Barley

SERVINGS: 5
PREP TIME: 10 min.
TOTAL TIME: 1 hour 10 min.

Ingredients

- 2 cups chicken broth
- 1 (15 ounce) can diced tomatoes
- 1/2 cup hulled barley
- 1/2 onion, diced
- 1/2 cup chopped mixed peppers
- 1 teaspoon paprika
- 1 teaspoon chili powder
- 1 teaspoon ground cumin

Instructions

1. In a rice cooker, combine chicken broth, diced tomatoes, barley, onion, peppers, paprika, chili powder, and cumin.
2. Cook according to rice cooker directions for 30 minutes. Stir and continue cooking until barley is tender, about 30 more minutes.

Romano Cheese Pasta

SERVINGS: 3
PREP TIME: 5 min.
TOTAL TIME: 25 min.

Ingredients

- 2 cups water or 2 cups broth, whichever you desire
- 1 cup tomato sauce
- 1/4 cup cooked ground beef or cooked hot sausage (optional)
- 1/4 teaspoon salt
- 1 teaspoon olive oil
- 1/8 teaspoon dried oregano
- 1/8 cup Romano cheese
- 2 cups uncooked rigatoni pasta or 2 cups penne

Instructions

1. Place all ingredients in rice cooker and stir. Add salt to taste.
2. Close lid and flip the switch to Cook. When cooker turns off, open and stir. Cover and leave on warm for 2 or 3 minutes or until ready to serve.

Meat Cabbage Casserole

SERVINGS: 6
PREP TIME: 15 min.
TOTAL TIME: 45 min.

Ingredients

- 1 medium head of cabbage, chopped
- 1 lb ground meat, browned and drained
- 1 lb sausage, sliced
- 1 can (6 ounce) tomato sauce
- 2 -3 whole tomatoes, cut up
- 1/2 cup onion, chopped
- 1/2 cup onion tops or 1/2 cup parsley
- 1 small bell pepper, chopped
- 1 cup uncooked rice
- 2 cups water
- salt and pepper

Instructions

1. Mix ingredients in rice cooker and cook until rice cooker goes off.
2. Serve warm.

SOUPS AND STEWS

Rice and Beef Soup

SERVINGS: 8
PREP TIME: 10 min.
TOTAL TIME: 1 hour 30 min

Ingredients

- 1 1/2 cups long grain rice
- 10 cups water
- 1 tablespoon fresh parsley, chopped
- 1 tablespoon fresh chives, chopped
- 1 tablespoon fresh rosemary, chopped
- salt and pepper
- 1/2 teaspoon cinnamon, ground
- 2 lbs beef, cubed

Instructions

1. Add rice, water, parsley, chives, rosemary, and pepper to a 10 cup or larger rice cooker (adjust all ingredients if rice cooker is smaller). Turn on rice cooker. Cover and cook.
2. When simmering, add the beef and cinnamon. Cover and press cook again.

Taco Soup

SERVINGS: 4
PREP/ TOTAL TIME: 50 min.

Ingredients

- 1/2 medium onion
- 1 garlic clove
- 1 tablespoon olive oil
- 3 chicken breasts
- 5 cups chicken broth, low-sodium
- 1 cup carrots, chopped
- 1 can diced tomatoes
- 1/2 cup brown rice, raw
- 1 cup corn, canned
- 1/2 cup black beans, canned

Instructions

3. Chop onion and garlic, and place in rice cooker with some oil. Press Cook and leave until it starts browning.
4. Chop chicken and add to rice cooker. Cook until browned.
5. Add chicken broth, chopped carrots, diced tomatoes, brown rice, corn, and black beans. Turn rice cooker to Brown Rice setting, if you don't have that setting Cook for at least 45 min-1 hour.

Chicken Chili

SERVINGS: 4
PREP/TOTAL TIME: 30 min.

Ingredients

- 1 lb. ground chicken
- 1 can black beans
- 1 can kidney beans
- 1 tablespoon chili powder
- 1 tablespoon tomato paste
- 1 cup tomato sauce (plain)
- 1/2 packet of chili seasoning
- 2 teaspoon dried oregano
- Salt and pepper, to taste

Instructions

1. Place raw ground chicken in rice cooker and press Cook. When chicken is browned and fully cooked through, drain the excess fat.
2. Combine beans, tomato sauce, and tomato paste in the cooker. Add in the seasonings and let simmer for another full cycle on the rice cooker.
3. Serve warm.

Turkey Barley Goulash Casserole

SERVINGS: 4
PREP TIME: 15 min.
TOTAL TIME: 45 min.

Ingredients

- 1 lb lean ground turkey or ground beef
- 1/2 cup chopped onion
- 1/4 cup chopped celery
- 1 red bell pepper, diced
- 1 carrot, shredded
- 3/4 cup barley
- 1 (6 ounce) can tomato paste
- 1 1/2 cups water
- 1 1/2 teaspoons salt
- 1/4 teaspoon pepper
- 1 garlic clove, minced
- 1 tablespoon Worcestershire sauce (optional)
- 2 tablespoons red wine (optional)
- 2 teaspoons sweet paprika (optional)

Instructions

1. Set rice cooker to Cook. Place the first five ingredients and cover. Every few minutes stir to break up clumps of turkey, and cover. When turkey is cooked, add rest of ingredients.
2. If you don't have the final three seasonings, you can leave them out or substitute with other desired seasonings. Close cover and set rice cooker to brown rice setting or just the Cook button if you don't have that setting.
3. Make sure barley is cooked through. If it is too chewy run through another cycle, about 40 minutes. If mixture is too dry, add more water.
4. Top with cheddar or parmesan cheese if desired.

Chicken & White Radish Soup

SERVINGS: 3
PREP TIME: 10 min.
TOTAL TIME: 1 1/2 hours

Ingredients

- 500 g chicken skin removed & chopped to smaller pieces
- 1 litre of water
- 5 slices of ginger
- 1 white radish(daikon) about 300g, peeled and cut to large chunks
- 8 shiitake mushrooms stems removed
- 1 tablespoon wolfberries soaked in water until puffy, drained
- 3 dried scallops
- salt to taste

Instructions

1. Add water to the rice cooker pot and set to Cook. When water is boiling, add chicken for 5-8 minutes with the rice cooker covered. Discard the cooking liquid and set aside the blanched chicken pieces.
2. Add a liter of water to the rice cooker. Cover and set to Cook. When the water is boiling, add chicken, daikon, mushrooms, dried scallops and ginger. Cover and return to a boil, leaving the soup in the Cook mode for about 45 minutes.
3. Switch to Warm and allow to simmer for at least another 1-2 hours.
4. Half an hour before serving, add the soaked wolfberries.
5. Add salt to taste and serve.

Desserts

Coconut-Pecan Upside Down Cake

SERVINGS: 4
PREP TIME: 5 min.
TOTAL TIME: 45 min

Ingredients

- 1/2 cup butter, softened
- 1/2 cup dark brown sugar
- 1/2 cup shredded coconut
- 2/3 cup chopped pecans
- 1/2 cup semi-sweet chocolate
- 2 tablespoons milk
- 1 (9 ounce) box of yellow cake mix or 0.5 (18 1/4 ounce) box cake mix

Instructions

1. Melt butter in rice cooker. Spray with cooking spray or use parchment paper on bottom of pan. Combine brown sugar, coconut, pecan's and semi-sweet chocolates with a bit of milk. Spread over the butter. Mix up cake mix according to the directions on the box.
2. Hit Cook, it should take around 40 minutes. Turn off and wait a few minutes before removing the pan from the rice cooker.
3. Turn cake over and allow to cool before cutting.

Chocolate Cake

SERVINGS: 12
PREP TIME: 5 min.
TOTAL TIME: 1 hour 5 min

Ingredients

- 1 1/2 cups white flour
- 1/2 cup raw sugar
- 4 tablespoons dark cocoa
- 1 teaspoon baking soda
- 1/2 teaspoon salt
- 1/2 teaspoon cinnamon
- 1/4 teaspoon double-acting baking powder
- 90 ml sunflower oil
- 1/2 teaspoon vanilla
- 1 tablespoon vinegar
- 1 cup water

Instructions

1. Add and mix together the dry ingredients. Add wet ingredients to the mixture, mixing well until smooth, around 1 minute. Pour batter into the greased rice cooker bowl.
2. Set rice cooker to Slow for 60 minutes, if it doesn't have one just use the regular Cook cycle. If rice cooker goes to Warm cycle, allow to be in that mode for a few minutes then restart timer for remainder time to equal 60 minutes total cook time. Check at 45 minutes.
3. When a toothpick comes out clean from edges and center of cake, it is cooked.
4. Take bowl out when cake is finished, and allow to cool for 15 minutes. Remove cake by inverting bowl on serving plate.
5. Sprinkle with powdered sugar or top with your favourite frosting.

Muffin Cake

SERVINGS: 8
PREP TIME: 15 min.
TOTAL TIME: 45 min.

Ingredients

- cooking spray
- 1 cup all-purpose flour
- 1/3 cup white sugar
- 2 teaspoons baking powder
- 1 teaspoon baking soda
- 1/4 teaspoon salt
- 1 1/2 cups bran flakes, crushed
- 1 cup skim milk
- 1 1/2 teaspoons ground cinnamon
- 1 1/2 teaspoons ground nutmeg
- 1 1/2 teaspoons vanilla extract
- 1 egg
- 1/4 cup olive oil
- 1/2 cup diced apple
- 1/2 cup diced banana
- 1/3 cup raisins

Instructions

1. Spray rice cooker bowl with cooking spray.
2. Mix flour, sugar, baking powder, baking soda, and salt in a bowl. In a separate large bowl, combine bran flakes, milk, cinnamon, nutmeg, and vanilla extract. Allow bran flakes to slightly absorb the milk, around 5 minutes. Add egg and oil to bran mix and stir. Combine flour in bran mix.
3. Gently fold apple, banana, and raisins in batter. Pour into rice cooker sprayed with cooking spray.
4. Cook in the rice cooker for three cycles or until a toothpick inserted in the center of the cake comes out clean, around 30 minutes.

Poached Pomegranate Spiced Pears

SERVINGS: 4
PREP TIME: 5 min.
TOTAL TIME: 2 hours

Ingredients

- 2 firm pears, peeled, halved, cored
- 2 cups pomegranate juice
- 2 cups apple cider
- 1- 3 inch cinnamon stick peel from one clementine
- 2 whole cloves
- 2 star anise
- 3 black cardamom pods
- 1-1 inch piece fresh ginger, peeled, cut into thin slivers
- Orange cashew cream for serving, if desired

Instructions

1. Place pomegranate juice, apple cider, cinnamon stick, clementine peel, cloves, star anise, cardamom pods and ginger in rice cooker. Poach pear halves in poaching liquid of choice.
2. Close rice cooker set to Cook for 50 minutes, or until a toothpick can easily go through. Open cover and turn pears over.
3. Let sit for an hour. Turn pears over again and let sit for another hour. Refrigerate overnight if you desire a more intense flavor and color.
4. Serve with Orange Cashew Cream, if desired.

Coconut Rice Pudding

SERVINGS: 8
PREP TIME: 5 min.
TOTAL TIME: 1 hour 5 min

Ingredients

- 2 cups Arborio rice or 2 cups short-grain rice
- 2 cups cold water
- 1 teaspoon salt
- 1/2 cup evaporated milk
- 1/2 cup coconut milk
- 1 cup sweetened condensed milk
- 1 cinnamon stick
- 1 lemon zest, one large piece of lemon peel
- 1/2 teaspoon nutmeg
- 3 tablespoons ground cinnamon, to garnish

Instructions

1. Measure short grain rice with rice cooker measuring cup, around 6 ounces or 3/4 of a cup. Rinse rice in cold water, and place rice, water and salt into rice cooker. Set to Cook and leave until it clicks to Warm. Turn off, stir, and let cool for 15 minutes.
2. In a separate bowl, whisk evaporated milk, coconut milk, sweetened condensed milk cinnamon stick, lemon zest, and nutmeg. Add the mix into the rice, cover and set the cooker to Warm setting. Check after 30 minutes to make sure consistency is to your liking.
3. Discard cinnamon stick and the lemon zest. Garnish with ground cinnamon and cream, if desired.

Quick & Easy
VEGETARIAN RICE COOKER
MEALS COOKBOOK

Over 50 recipes for breakfast, main dishes, and desserts

By Susan Evans

BREAKFAST

Frittata with Summer Vegetables

SERVINGS: 4
PREP TIME: 5 min.
TOTAL TIME: 50 min

Ingredients

- 1 whole garlic clove, peeled
- 1 small red or yellow pepper, cut into small dice
- 1 small potato, peeled and finely julienned
- 1 small zucchini, sliced into thin rounds salt and pepper
- 1 tablespoon olive oil
- 6 large eggs
- 2 tablespoons grated cheese of any kind (optional)
- salt and pepper
- 1 tablespoon olive oil

Instructions

1. Heat frying pan with 1 tablespoon of olive oil. Add garlic clove and cook until garlic is lightly brown. Discard the garlic clove. Add the vegetables. Season with salt and pepper and set aside.
2. Put 1 tablespoon of olive oil in the rice cooker. Spread it around the bottom and up the sides with a paper towel. Add eggs, grated cheese, salt and pepper, and beat the eggs in the bowl (avoid scratching the rice cooker). Add the vegetables and distribute evenly in the egg mixture.
3. Put bowl in rice cooker and switch to Cook.
4. When it finishes cooking, let cool completely and cut into wedges.

Vanilla Almond Steel-Cut Oatmeal

SERVINGS: 3
PREP TIME: 10 min.
TOTAL TIME: 40 min.

Ingredients

- 1 cup steel-cut oats
- 2 cups unsweetened, original soy milk
- 1 1/2 cup water
- 2 teaspoons vanilla extract
- 1/2 teaspoon salt
- raw sliced almonds
- brown sugar
- maple syrup

Instructions

1. Add oatmeal, soymilk, water, vanilla extract, and salt to rice cooker. Set to porridge setting or regular Cook setting.
2. Add toppings and serve.

Avocado Breakfast Bowl

SERVINGS: 2
PREP TIME: 10 min.
TOTAL TIME: 30 min.

Ingredients

- 1/2 cup water
- 1/4 cup red quinoa
- 1 1/2 teaspoons olive oil
- 2 eggs
- 1 pinch salt and ground black pepper to taste
- 1/4 teaspoon seasoned salt
- 1/4 teaspoon ground black pepper
- 1 avocado, diced
- 2 tablespoons crumbled feta cheese

Instructions

1. Combine water and quinoa together in a rice cooker. Cook until quinoa is tender, around 15 minutes.
2. Heat olive oil in a skillet over medium heat. Cook eggs as desired an; season with salt and pepper.
3. Combine quinoa and eggs in a bowl.
4. Top with avocado and feta cheese.

Rice Cooker Oatmeal

SERVINGS: 3
PREP TIME: 5 min.
TOTAL TIME: 30 min.

Ingredients

- 1 1/4 cups large flake rolled oats
- 2 tablespoons wheat bran
- 1 pinch salt
- 1/3 cup raisins or 1/3 cup fresh or dried fruit (optional)
- 2 1/2 cups water

Instructions

1. Put all ingredients in a rice cooker and turn on. It should be done around 25 to 30 minutes. Stir once during cooking.
2. Sprinkle with some ground flaxseed, sugar, and light cream; if desired.

Creamy Grits

SERVINGS: 2
PREP TIME: 5 min.
TOTAL TIME: 30 min.

Ingredients

- 1/2 cup stone-ground grits
- 1 1/2 cups milk
- 1/4 teaspoon salt
- 1 tablespoon butter
- Spoonful of cherry

Instructions

1. Put all ingredients into rice cooker bowl and combine. Set to Cook. Stir after 10 minutes into cycle.
2. Serve with a pat of butter and a spoonful of cherry or other preserves.

Steel Cut Oats

SERVINGS: 4
PREP TIME: 5 min.
TOTAL TIME: 25 min.

Ingredients

- 1 part steel cut oats
- 3 parts water
- pinch of salt

Instructions

1. Put oats, water and salt in rice cooker. Try to add up to half the capacity of rice cooker, since oats bubble up more than rice.
2. Start rice cooker.

Creamy Oatmeal

SERVINGS: 2
PREP TIME: 5 min.
TOTAL TIME: 30 min

Ingredients

- 2/3 cup steel cut oats
- 1 2/3 cups milk
- 1 teaspoon pure vanilla extract
- 1 1/4 teaspoons ground cinnamon
- 1 pinch fine sea salt
- 2 tablespoons pure maple syrup
- 1/2 cup chopped dates

Instructions

1. Place all ingredients except dates, in rice cooker. Gently stir to combine and sprinkle dates on top. Cover and set on Porridge cycle, or set to Cook if rice cooker doesn't have one. Watch to determine when the oatmeal is done, around 25 to 30 minutes.

Tapioca Pudding

SERVINGS: 4
PREP TIME: 5 min.
TOTAL TIME: 25 min

Ingredients

- 3 tablespoons small pearl tapioca
- 2 cups milk
- 1 large egg
- 1/2 cup sugar
- 1 pinch salt
- 1 teaspoon pure vanilla extract

Instructions

1. Place tapioca in rice cooker. In a small bowl, whisk together milk, egg, sugar, and salt. Pour milk mix over the tapioca and stir to combine. Cover and set to Porridge cycle or to Cook for 20 minutes.
2. When it switches to Warm cycle, remove bowl from cooker and stir in vanilla. Pour pudding into a large bowl or individual dishes.
3. Let cool.
4. Serve warm, if desired, or refrigerate covered with plastic wrap.

Rice Dishes

Dill and Lemon Rice with Feta

SERVINGS: 3
PREP TIME: 5 min.
TOTAL TIME: 45 min.

Ingredients

- 1 1/2 cups long grain white rice
- 2 cups vegetable stock
- 2 tablespoons olive oil
- 2 small boiling onions, chopped
- 1/4 cup pine nuts
- 1/4 cup fresh lemon juice
- 1 tablespoon minced fresh dill
- 1 1/2 teaspoons minced of fresh mint, optional
- 1 cup crumbled feta
- 1 lemon, cut in 8 wedges

Instructions

1. Coat rice bowl with cooking spray. Add rice and stock. Set for the regular white rice cycle.
2. When it switches to Warm, let stand and steam for 10 minutes.
3. Heat olive oil in a small skillet. Add onions and cook for 5 minutes, frequently stirring until soft. Add pine nuts. Cook and stir until golden, about a minute.
4. Add the onion and pine nut mixture to the rice, along with the lemon juice, dill, and mint (if using). Stir with a plastic rice paddle or a wooden spoon to combine.
5. Cover and continue on Warm setting for 10 more minutes.
6. Transfer to a serving dish, and top with the feta and lemon wedges.

Spanish Rice

SERVINGS: 8
PREP TIME: 10 min.
TOTAL TIME: 40 min

Ingredients

- 2 cups long grain rice
- 1 cup water
- 1 (8 ounce) can tomato sauce
- 14 ounces Mexican-style stewed tomatoes, with juice
- 1/4 cup salsa
- 3/4 teaspoon cumin
- 2 teaspoons chili powder
- 3/4 teaspoon garlic salt
- 1 1/2 teaspoons dried onion
- 3/4 teaspoon salt, optional
- 1/2 cup water
- 1 small green pepper, diced, optional
- 1 (4 ounce) can diced green chilies, optional

Instructions

1. Spray rice cooker with cooking spray. Add and stir in rice, 1 cup water, and all other ingredients.
2. When the cycle is almost completed check the rice and add additional 1/2 cup water if necessary. The amount of water will differ depending on what kind of rice you use.
3. Serve warm.

Fragrant Basmati Rice

SERVINGS: 3
PREP TIME: 15 min.
TOTAL TIME: 35 min.

Ingredients

- 1 cup basmati rice
- 1 1/2 cups water
- 1/4 teaspoon salt
- 1 cinnamon stick (4 inches)
- 3 green cardamom pods

Instructions

1. Rinse the rice and thoroughly drain. Place all ingredients in the rice cooker and stir to combine. Set regular Cook cycle.
2. When the machine shifts to Warm, set a timer for 15 minutes. When done, fluff rice with the plastic or wooden paddle/spoon.
3. Serve warm.

Carrots and Peas Rice

SERVINGS: 6
PREP TIME: 10 min.
TOTAL TIME: 35 min.

Ingredients

- 2 tablespoons unsalted butter, divided
- 1/4 cup carrot, sliced in rounds
- 1 1/2 cups long grain white rice (or any flavorful white rice)
- 2 cups vegetable stock
- 1 tablespoon fresh Italian parsley, chopped
- 1 teaspoon dried thyme
- 1/4 cup frozen peas
- 1 tablespoon almonds, chopped

Instructions

1. In a small skillet over medium heat, melt 1 tablespoon of butter. Add the carrots stir and cook, until softened, around 2-3 minutes.
2. Place rice in rice cooker. Add and stir in stock, parsley, thyme, peas and sautéed carrots. Close cover and press Cook. When machine switches to Warm, let rice steam for 10 minutes.
3. Fluff rice with wooden spoon. When ready to serve, add 1 tablespoon of butter and almonds. Stir and immediately serve.

Lemon Rice

SERVINGS: 4
PREP/ TOTAL TIME: 45 min.

Ingredients

- 1 cup long grain rice
- 1 1/2 cups vegetable stock
- 1 pinch salt
- 1 large garlic clove
- 2 teaspoons lemon zest, freshly grated
- 2 tablespoons unsalted butter
- 2 tablespoons fresh Italian parsley

Instructions

1. Place rinsed rice in the rice cooker bowl. Add chicken stock and salt and stir to combine. Place the garlic on top of the rice in the center.
2. Close the cover and set to Cook. When it switches to the Warm, add and stir in lemon zest, butter, and parsley. Close cover and let the rice steam for 10 minutes. Fluff with a rice paddle.
3. Before serving, remove and discard garlic. Serve hot.

Orange Chipotle Risotto

SERVINGS: 6
PREP TIME: 10 min.
TOTAL TIME: 45 min.

Ingredients

- 1 tablespoon butter
- 1 small onion (about 1 cup)
- 1 cup Arborio rice
- 3 cups hot water, adding more if needed
- 1 cup orange juice
- 1/2 teaspoon orange zest
- 1 teaspoon saffron thread, optional
- 1 chipotle chile in adobo, to taste
- 3 ounces asiago cheese, 1/2 cup grated
- 1 bunch fresh parsley, 1/4 cup chopped

Instructions

1. Sauté onions in butter in an open rice cooker.
2. Add Arborio rice and liquids, zest, saffron, and chipotle pepper and sauce. Set to Cook.
3. Mix in grated cheese and herbs after it has switched to Warm cycle.
4. Season to taste with salt and pepper.

Moroccan Brown Rice

SERVINGS: 4
PREP TIME: 5 min.
TOTAL TIME: 45 min.

Ingredients

- 1 1/2 cups long grain brown rice
- 2 3/4 cups water or 2 3/4 cups vegetable stock
- 3/4 teaspoon salt
- 1/2 teaspoon pepper
- 1 teaspoon ground coriander
- 1/2 teaspoon ground cardamom
- 3 tablespoons butter, cut into pieces
- 1/4 cup preserved lemon, minced, garnish

Instructions

1. Coat rice cooker bowl with cooking spray. Place rice in the bowl and add water, salt, pepper, coriander and cardamom.
2. Cover and set the Brown rice cycle. Add the butter when the machine switches to Warm.
3. Cover and let rice steam for 10 minutes.
4. Fluff rice and serve hot. Sprinkled some preserved lemon.

Rice Pilaf

SERVINGS: 7
PREP TIME: 10 min.
TOTAL TIME: 25 min

Ingredients

- 1 1/2 cups white rice
- 2 cups vegetable broth
- 1/4 cup slivered almonds
- 1 cup sliced mushrooms
- 1/2 small onion, diced
- 2 teaspoons margarine or 2 teaspoons butter
- 2 teaspoons minced garlic cloves

Instructions

1. In a small frying pan, sauté onion and garlic over medium heat until onion is translucent.
2. Add rice, sautéed onion and garlic, almonds, mushrooms, and broth to rice cooker. Stir and set to cook.
3. When finished cooking, let sit for 10 minutes.

Mexican Rice

SERVINGS: 6
PREP/TOTAL TIME: 25 min.

Ingredients

- 1 cup rice
- 2 1/4 cups low sodium vegetable broth
- 6 ounce tomato paste
- 2 tablespoons butter
- 1/2 cup onion, diced
- 1 garlic clove, small, minced
- 4 ounces diced green chilies
- 1 dash pepper
- 1 dash red pepper flakes
- cilantro or parsley

Instructions

1. Combine and stir in ingredients in rice cooker. Press cook.
2. When cooking is finished let stand uncovered for 3 minutes.
3. Stir before serving.

Italian Rice and Peas

SERVINGS: 5
PREP TIME: 15 min.
TOTAL TIME: 35 min.

Ingredients

- 1 tablespoon olive oil
- 1 tablespoon unsalted butter
- 1/2 cup shallot, minced
- 1/2 cup celery, minced
- 2 tablespoons dry white wine
- 1 cup medium-grain risotto rice
- 2 tablespoons medium-grain risotto rice
- 3 cups chicken stock or 3 cups meat stock or 3 cups vegetable stock
- 1 1/2 cups peas (fresh or frozen)
- 2 teaspoons unsalted butter
- 2 tablespoons heavy cream
- 1/4 cup parmesan cheese

Instructions

1. Set rice cooker to Cook. Place olive oil and butter in rice cooker. When butter melts, add shallots and celery. Cook until the shallots are softened but not browned, 2 to 3 minutes, stirring occasionally. Add wine and cook for a few minutes. Add rice and stir to coat grains with the hot butter.
2. Cook until rice grains are transparent except for a white spot on each, 3-5 minutes stirring occasionally. Add stock and peas (if fresh), stirring to combine.
3. Close cover and set to Cook. When the machine switches to Warm cycle, stir rice with a plastic or wooden rice paddle. The rice should be al dente.
4. Cook for a few minutes longer if needed. When ready to serve, add peas (if frozen or very tender fresh ones) and stir to combine.
5. Add butter and close the lid for 2-3 minutes to allow butter to melt and the peas are heated through. Stir in cream, cheese, and salt to taste.
6. Serve immediately.

Caribbean Rice

SERVINGS: 4
PREP TIME: 15 min.
TOTAL TIME: 40 min.

Ingredients

- 1 cup white rice, rinsed
- 1 teaspoon ground Jamaican jerk spice or seasoning
- 1/4 cup cilantro or 1/4 cup parsley
- 1 sprig thyme, stem discarded
- 1 garlic clove, minced
- 1 teaspoon grated fresh ginger
- 2 scallions, sliced
- 3/4 cup finely diced sweet potato
- 1/3 cup toasted coconut
- 1/3 cup raisins
- 1/3 cup diced red pepper
- 1 cup vegetable broth, to cover rice

Instructions

1. Place all the ingredients in rice cooker, except for 1 tablespoon scallions and 1 teaspoon coconut which should be saved for garnish. Pour broth 3/4 inch above the level of the rice. Press the cook button.
2. When cooked, fluff with fork. Place in a serving dish and top with reserved coconut and scallions. Place lime alongside for garnish.

Mexican Green Rice

SERVINGS: 4
PREP TIME: 10 min.
TOTAL TIME: 55 min.

Ingredients

- 1 tablespoon unsalted butter
- 1/2 small white onion, chopped
- 1 cup long grain white rice
- 1 1/2 cups water
- 1/2 teaspoon salt
- 1/2 cup fresh cilantro leaves, minced

Instructions

1. Set rice cooker to Cook or regular/Brown Rice cycle. Place butter in rice cooker bowl. When melted, add the onion. Cook and stir until onion is softened and translucent, about 5 minutes. Add rice, water, salt and cilantro to the rice cooker bowl. Stir to combine.
2. Close cover and reset for the regular/Brown Rice cycle or allow previous cycle to complete.
3. When the machine switches over to the Warm cycle, let the rice steam for 15 minutes.
4. Fluff rice with wooden or plastic rice paddle. Serve hot.

Easy Coconut Rice

SERVINGS: 4
PREP TIME: 5 min.
TOTAL TIME: 35 min.

Ingredients

- 2 cups coconut milk
- 2 3/4 cups water
- 2 cups rice
- 1 teaspoon salt

Instructions

1. Clean and wash the rice. Place all ingredients in rice cooker and set to Cook.
2. After it switches to warm, let stand 10 minutes to steam.
3. Serve warm.

Vegetable Rice Pilaf

SERVINGS: 6
PREP TIME: 20 min.
TOTAL TIME: 1 hour 10 min

Ingredients

- 3 teaspoons vegetable bouillon granules
- 3 1/2 cups water
- 3 cups uncooked white rice
- 4 small heads baby bok choy, trimmed and chopped
- 3 green onions, chopped
- 1 carrot, chopped
- 4 mushrooms, chopped
- 1 teaspoon vegetable bouillon granules
- 1/4 cup water, or more if needed
- ground black pepper to taste

Instructions

1. In the rice cooker, dissolve 3 teaspoons bouillon in 3 1/2 cups water.
2. Stir rice, baby bok choy, green onions, carrot, and mushrooms into the bouillon and water mixture.
3. Start rice cooker and cook until liquid is absorbed and rice is tender, around 50 minutes.
4. In a small bowl dissolve 1 teaspoon bouillon and 1/4 cup water. Transfer mixture to a blender.
5. Scoop about 1 cup of the rice mixture into the blender with the bouillon mixture. Blend until mixture becomes a thin paste. Add more water as needed.
6. Mix rice paste with remaining cooked vegetables and rice until thoroughly combined.
7. Season with black pepper.

Quick and Easy Spinach Rice

SERVINGS: 4
PREP TIME: 10 min.
TOTAL TIME: 45 min

Ingredients

- 1 tablespoon vegetable oil, or as needed
- 1 teaspoon cumin seeds
- 1 small onion, minced
- 1 large carrot, minced
- 4 green chile peppers, chopped
- 1 teaspoon ginger-garlic paste
- 1 1/2 cups fresh spinach
- 2 cups uncooked white rice
- 1 teaspoon roasted coriander powder
- 1 pinch salt, or to taste
- 4 1/2 cups water, or more as needed

Instructions

1. Heat oil over medium heat in a skillet. Add and stir cumin seeds until fragrant, about 1 minute. Add onion, carrot, and green chile peppers. Cook and stir until slightly tender, about 5 minutes. Add ginger-garlic powder and cook for about 5 minutes.
2. In a blender, pulse spinach leaves until it turns into a paste. Add spinach paste to onion mixture. Cook and stir until water has evaporated from the spinach, about 2 to 3 minutes.
3. Mix and combine rice, coriander powder, and salt into spinach mixture. Transfer rice mixture to a rice cooker and add water. Press the Cook button.

Chile Cheese Rice

SERVINGS: 8
PREP TIME: 10 min.
TOTAL TIME: 25 min.

Ingredients

- 2 cups white rice, using rice cooker cups
- 3 cups water or 3 cups vegetable broth
- 1 (4 ounce) can diced green chilies
- 1/2 medium onion, diced
- 2 teaspoons garlic
- 1 cup Monterey jack cheese, shredded
- 1 tablespoon margarine

Instructions

1. Sauté onion and garlic in margarine in a small saucepan over medium heat, until onion becomes translucent.
2. Place rice, sautéed onion and garlic, chilies, and chicken broth in rice cooker. Stir to combine. Set cooker to Cook setting. When cooked, mix in shredded cheese and let sit 5-10 minutes.

Toasted Coconut Yellow Rice

SERVINGS: 8
PREP TIME: 10 min.
TOTAL TIME: 45 min.

Ingredients

- 2 cups white rice, thoroughly rinsed
- 1 (14 ounce) can coconut milk
- 1 1/4 cups water
- 1/4 cup sweetened flaked coconut, divided
- 1 teaspoon ground turmeric
- 1/2 teaspoon kosher salt

Instructions

1. Place rinsed rice into rice cooker.
2. Combine and stir coconut milk, water, half of the flaked coconut, turmeric, and salt in a small saucepan. Place over medium-high heat and cook until turmeric is dissolved in the milk mixture and the color is uniform. Pour coconut milk mixture over the rice.
3. Press Start and cook until the cycle completes, about 25 minutes. Leave rice on Warm for 5 minutes.
4. Heat a small skillet over medium-high heat. Toast remaining coconut in skillet until golden brown, about 5 minutes.
5. Fluff cooked rice. Sprinkle toasted coconut over the rice and serve.

Wild Berry Rice

SERVINGS: 4
PREP TIME: 5 min.
TOTAL TIME: 25 min.

Ingredients

- 1 1/2 cups short-grain white rice
- 2 cups water
- 45 ml honey, warmed
- 2 tablespoons butter, melted
- 1 cup cream
- 1 cup mixed berry (fresh or frozen)
- 1/4 cup icing sugar
- 1/4 cup water
- 2 tablespoons port wine (optional)
- berries, for serving

Instructions

1. Place rice and 2 cups water into rice cooker. Cover and set on Cook.
2. Fluff rice and stir in honey, butter and cream. Close lid and allow to stand to for 10 minutes on Warm setting.
3. In a food processer place berries, icing sugar, 1/4 cup water and port and process until smooth. Fold berry mix through rice mix.
4. Transfer to serving glasses and top with extra berries and cream.

Brown Rice with Miso

SERVINGS: 4
PREP TIME: 2 min.
TOTAL TIME: 35 min

Ingredients

- 1 1/2 tablespoons miso (white or yellow)
- 2 1/4 cups water or 2 1/4 cups vegetable stock
- 1 inch fresh gingerroot, peeled
- 2 teaspoons lemon juice
- 1 cup brown rice

Instructions

1. Dissolve miso in 1/4 cup of the water. Combine dissolved miso and the rest of the ingredients in the rice cooker bowl.
2. Set to brown rice or regular Cook cycle. When it switches to Warm cycle, let stand for 15 minutes. Then fluff rice with the plastic paddle or a wooden spoon.
3. Discard ginger and serve.

Saffron & Fruit Chutney Yellow Rice

SERVINGS: 6
PREP/TOTAL TIME: 5 min.
TOTAL TIME: 35 min.

Ingredients

- 3 cups basmati rice, rinsed
- 3 cups water, to the rice cooker level
- 1 pinch powdered saffron (about 5 - 8 strands) or 1 pinch saffron strand (about 5 - 8 strands)
- 2 tablespoons fruit chutney
- 2 -4 cardamom pods, split & use seeds
- salt and pepper
- 1 ounce butter
- 2 -4 sprigs fresh coriander, optional

Instructions

1. Place 3 cups of rinsed Basmati rice in rice cooker, using cup provided. Fill up with water to the 3 cup level. Add saffron, cardamom seeds, salt, pepper & chutney to the rice and water. Using the special non-stick spatula, gently mix. Turn on to the Cook cycle.
2. When ready to serve, add the butter and gently combine. Garnish with chopped fresh coriander/cilantro. Top with some toasted flaked almonds.

Sushi Rice

SERVINGS: 12
PREP TIME: 20 min.
TOTAL TIME: 35 min.

Ingredients

- 3 cups medium grain rice
- 3 1/4 cups water
- 1/3 cup seasoned rice vinegar (to taste)

Instructions

1. Place rice and water in rice cooker. Push button to start cooking.
2. After it is done cooking and it switches to warm, let rice sit in the cooker for about 15 minutes without opening the lid to allow complete steaming. Put rice into a separate bowl and pour vinegar over rice. Gently toss and mix with rice paddle, careful not to mash the rice grains.
3. Use in rolls, sushi or to accompany sashimi.

Rice and Black Beans

SERVINGS: 4
PREP TIME: 5 min.
TOTAL TIME: 35 min.

Ingredients

- 1 cup uncooked rice
- 1 can (10 ounce) diced tomatoes with green chilies (Rotel)
- 1 can (14 1/2 ounce) vegetable broth
- 1 can (15 1/4 ounce) black beans
- 1 can (14 3/4 ounce) sweet corn (optional)
- 1 cup cheese (optional)

Instructions

1. Drain tomatoes, black beans, and corn. Place in rice cooker. Add rice, chicken broth and stir. Cook until cooker stops.
2. Top with cheese and serve.

Easy Jambalaya Curry

SERVINGS: 4
PREP TIME: 5 min.
TOTAL TIME: 50 min.

Ingredients

- 2 tablespoons oil
- 1 cup chopped onion
- 1 tablespoon minced garlic
- 2 tablespoons curry powder
- 2 cups water
- 1 (8 ounce) can tomato sauce
- 1 (8 ounce) package jambalaya mix
- 1/2 cup golden raisin
- 3/4 cup plain yogurt
- 1/3 cup chopped cashews

Instructions

1. Hit Cook and place oil in rice cooker. Add onion and garlic; and cook and stir 5 minutes or until onion is tender. Add curry powder. Cook and stir another 2 minutes.
2. Add water, tomato sauce, Jambalaya Mix, and raisins mix well. Close Lid and hit Cook. After cooker switches to Warm, turn off the cooker and stir in yogurt.
3. Let stand 5 minutes. Sprinkle with cashews.

Polynesian Rice

SERVINGS: 4
PREP TIME: 10 min.
TOTAL TIME: 45 min.

Ingredients

- 1 cup long grain rice
- 1 1/2 cups water
- 1 tablespoon water
- 1/4 teaspoon salt
- 1/4 teaspoon pepper
- 2 teaspoons curry powder
- 1 green onion, minced
- 1/2 cup pineapple, chopped
- 1 cup seedless grapes
- 1/4 cup green bell pepper, seeded and minced
- 1 cup cucumber, diced, for garnish
- 1 lime, cut into wedges, for garnish

Instructions

1. Spray rice cooker bowl with cooking spray or coat with vegetable oil.
2. Put first 6 ingredients (rice to curry powder) in rice cooker. Stir with paddle. Cover and set for regular Cook cycle.
3. When rice cooker switches to Warm, sprinkle green onion, pineapple, grapes (or cherries), and green pepper on top. Cover and let steam for 15 minutes. Stir rice with plastic rice paddle.
4. Garnish with cucumber and lime wedges. Serve.

Quick and Easy Curry Rice

SERVINGS: 5
PREP TIME: 5 min.
TOTAL TIME: 20 min.

Ingredients

- 2 cups uncooked white rice, rinsed
- 3 cups water
- 3 tablespoons mild curry powder

Instructions

1. Stir rice, water, and curry powder together in rice cooker. Cook for a full cycle or until all water is absorbed, about 15 to 20 minutes.

NON-RICE DISHES

Rice Cooker Mac & Cheese

SERVINGS: 4
PREP TIME: 5 min.
TOTAL TIME: 40 min.

Ingredients

- 2 cups pasta
- 1 1/2 cups vegetable stock
- 1 teaspoon salt
- 1 cup whole milk
- 1 1/2 cups shredded cheese

Instructions

1. Place the first three ingredients in the rice cooker and cook for 15 minutes.
2. Add milk and cheese, stir to combine. Close lid and cook for an additional 20 minutes
3. Serve warm.

Very Cheesy Polenta

SERVINGS: 4
PREP TIME: 10 min.
TOTAL TIME: 40 min.

Ingredients

- 2 tablespoons butter
- 1/2 onion, chopped
- 1 clove garlic, minced
- 1 cup vegetable broth
- 1 cup milk
- 1/2 cup polenta
- 1/4 teaspoon salt, or more to taste
- 2 ounces shredded Cheddar cheese
- 2 ounces shredded Parmesan cheese
- 1/4 teaspoon freshly ground black pepper

Instructions

1. Place butter, onion, and garlic in rice cooker. Cover and set cooker on. Cook until onion is soft and translucent, about 10 to 15 minutes, stirring occasionally.
2. Add broth, milk, polenta, and salt. Cover and cook on full cycle, occasionally stirring until polenta absorbs the liquid, around 20 minutes.
3. Add Cheddar cheese, Parmesan cheese, and black pepper. Stir until cheese is melted.

Steamed Tofu & Asparagus

SERVINGS: 4
PREP TIME: 15 min.
TOTAL TIME: 35 min.

Ingredients

- 1/2 small asparagus bunch, 1 1/2-inch lengths
- 1/2 (6 oz.) fried tofu, cubed
- 1/2 small carrot, peeled, thinly sliced
- 1 clove garlic, minced
- 1 tablespoon Aloha Shoyu
- 1 teaspoon vegetable oil
- 1 teaspoon sesame seed oil
- 1 teaspoon mirin
- 1 teaspoon honey

Instructions

1. Toss and combine all ingredients in rice cooker. Turn on rice cooker to cook.

Southwest-Style Quinoa

SERVINGS: 10
PREP TIME: 10 min.
TOTAL TIME: 1 hour 10 min.

Ingredients

- 2 cans (15 ounce) black beans, rinsed and drained
- 2 cans (10 ounce) diced tomatoes with green chile peppers, undrained
- 1 box (12 ounce) quinoa
- 2 cups water
- 1 package (1.25 ounce) dry taco seasoning mix

Instructions

1. Combine black beans, diced tomatoes with green chile peppers, quinoa, water, and taco seasoning in a rice cooker.
2. Cook quinoa mixture on the "brown rice" setting if you have it, or just the regular Cook setting, about 1 hour.

Kimchi

SERVINGS: 4
PREP/ TOTAL TIME: 3 days

Ingredients

- 1 small Napa cabbage (1 lb), cut in half and sliced into 1/2 inch slices
- 1 daikon radish, julienned
- 6 Thai chiles, minced
- 2 cloves garlic, minced
- 1/2 cup green onions, cut into 1/2 inch pieces
- 2 tablespoons ginger, grated
- 1/2 cup coarse sea salt
- 2 tablespoons unseasoned rice vinegar
- 1 teaspoon sugar

Instructions

1. Fill the rice cooker with 2 cups of water and add the salt. Add cabbage and stir making sure it is well coated. Cover and let sit for 24 hours, occasionally stirring.
2. Drain cabbage and add in the rest of the ingredients. Transfer to an airtight canning jar and seal well. Let sit for 3 days at room temperature. Make sure cabbage is covered with pickling liquid by turning upside down.

Rice Cooker Quinoa

SERVINGS: 4
PREP TIME: 2 min.
TOTAL TIME: 20 min.

Ingredients

- 1 cup quinoa
- 2 cups liquid (low-sodium vegetable broth, or water)
- 1/2 teaspoon salt

Instructions

1. Rinse 1 cup of quinoa in cold water. Pour rinsed quinoa into rice cooker.
2. Add liquid and salt. Turn on your rice cooker.
3. Allow quinoa to set for 3 to 5 minutes. Fluff with a fork and serve.

Cheesy Paprika Mac 'n Cheese

SERVINGS: 3
PREP TIME: 10 min.
TOTAL TIME: 40 min.

Ingredients

- 1 1/2 cups elbow macaroni
- 1 1/2 cups vegetable broth
- 1 cup unsweetened almond milk
- 3/4 cup shredded Cheddar cheese
- 1/2 cup shredded mozzarella cheese
- 1/4 cup grated Parmesan cheese
- 1/4 teaspoon paprika
- salt and ground black pepper, to taste

Instructions

1. Mix macaroni, broth, and almond milk together in the rice cooker. Press the Cook button until macaroni is tender yet firm to the bite, around 30 to 40 minutes.
2. Stir Cheddar cheese, mozzarella cheese, Parmesan cheese, paprika, salt, and pepper into macaroni mix until cheeses are melted.

Pasta Cubano

SERVINGS: 3
PREP TIME: 15 min.
TOTAL TIME: 25 min

Ingredients

- 1 tablespoon olive oil
- 400 grams ground round
- 1 cup minced red or green bell peppers
- 1/2 cup minced onions salt, to taste
- 1 teaspoon ground cumin
- 1 teaspoon dried oregano
- 2 tablespoons Worcestershire sauce
- 2 cups water
- 1 cup canned diced tomatoes
- 2 tablespoons sliced green olives
- 1 teaspoon olive oil
- 2 cups uncooked elbow macaroni or penne
- grated Parmesan cheese, for topping

Instructions

1. Heat olive oil in a medium pan. Add ground round and cook until browned. Add and sauté bell peppers and minced onions, until fragrant and soft. Season with salt, cumin, and oregano. Remove from heat. Add Worcestershire sauce.
2. Transfer beef mixture to the rice cooker. Add and mix in water, diced tomatoes, olives, olive oil, and uncooked pasta. Turn on the rice cooker.
3. Check the pasta when it switches to the warm setting. If pasta is not yet cooked, add more water and turn the rice cooker on again.
4. To avoid the pasta becoming soft, do not leave the rice cooker on warm for a long time.
5. Once pasta is al dente, transfer to serving plate and top with cheese.

Quinoa Pomegranate salad

SERVINGS: 4
PREP/ TOTAL TIME: 35 min.

Ingredients

- 2 cups quinoa, rinsed
- 4 cups water pinch of salt
- 1 cup pomegranate seeds
- 1/2 teaspoon all spice powder
- 1/2 cup chopped fresh mint
- 1 tablespoon pine nuts, toasted
- squeeze of lemon juice
- 1 teaspoon olive oil
- salt and cracked black pepper, to taste

Instructions

1. Place quinoa, water and a pinch of salt in the rice cooker. Turn it on.
2. Toast pine nuts while you wait.
3. When quinoa is done, combine all spice and lemon juice. Let it cool.
4. Add all other ingredients and combine.

Potato Salad

SERVINGS: 6
PREP TIME: 10 min.
TOTAL TIME: 30 min. + refrigeration

Ingredients

- 1 1/2 lbs small potatoes
- 1 1/2 cups water, for rice cooker
- 1 1/2 cups mayonnaise
- 1 tablespoon extra-virgin olive oil
- 1 -2 tablespoon vinegar
- 1 teaspoon celery seed
- 2 tablespoons chopped onions
- 1 -2 stalk celery, chopped
- 2 teaspoons prepared mustard
- 1 -2 tablespoon pickle relish
- 1/2 teaspoon salt, to taste
- 2 -4 hard-boiled eggs, coarsely chopped
- Paprika, for garnish

Instructions

1. Cut potatoes into bite size pieces and place in rice cooker with water. Turn rice cooker on Cook and cook for 10-15 minutes, or until potatoes are done.
2. Place rice cooker pan in sink and run cold water in the pan to cool potatoes and eggs. Drain well.
3. Put potatoes in a bowl or container and add the rest of the ingredients. Combine well and refrigerate.

Black Bean Chili

SERVINGS: 6
PREP TIME: 10 min.
TOTAL TIME: 55 min.

Ingredients

- 1 tablespoon olive oil
- 2 carrots diced
- 1/2 onion diced
- 2 cloves crushed garlic
- 2 cans black beans, drained and rinsed
- 1 can black beans, undrained
- 2 tablespoons chili powder
- 1 tablespoon cumin
- 1 can vegetarian refried black beans
- 1 large can of chopped tomatoes
- 1 cup vegetable broth
- pinch of salt
- shredded cheddar
- chopped avocado

Instructions

1. In large pot over medium heat, sauté onions and olive oil and cook until translucent. Add carrots and garlic, and cook until carrots soften. Transfer to a rice cooker and add broth, tomatoes, cumin and chili powder. Start your rice cooker.
2. After it has cooked, add black beans and cook for another cook cycle. When the second cycle is done, add refried beans and combine. Leave rice cooker on Warm to allow refried beans to come up to temperature.
3. Serve with cheddar cheese and avocado.

Rice Cooker Polenta

SERVINGS: 4
PREP TIME: 5 min.
TOTAL TIME: 20 min.

Ingredients

- 1 cup cornmeal (polenta)
- 3 cups water
- 1/4 cup parmesan cheese, grated
- 3 green onions, finely chopped, optional
- 1 tablespoon olive oil
- 1/2 teaspoon oregano
- 1/2 teaspoon basil
- 1/2 teaspoon thyme
- 1/4 teaspoon marjoram
- 1/4 teaspoon sage

Instructions

1. Place all ingredients in rice cooker. Start cooking cycle.
2. After cycle is complete, wait 10 minutes and allow polenta to absorb all the liquid.
3. Stir well before serving.

Rice Cooker Quinoa

SERVINGS: 2
PREP/TOTAL TIME: 20 min.

Ingredients

- 3/4 cup quinoa
- water
- 2 drops olive oil
- salt (suggested 1/4 of a tea spoon)

Instructions

1. Place quinoa in rice cooker. Fill with filtered water per rice cooker instruction.
2. Add olive oil and salt.
3. Set to Cook until it switches to Warm setting.

Jamaican Grits

SERVINGS: 2
PREP TIME: 5 min.
TOTAL TIME: 40 min.

Ingredients

- 16 ounces hominy
- 2 cups water
- 1/2 cup grits
- 1 cup cheese
- 1 teaspoon salt
- 1/4 teaspoon garlic powder
- 2 ounces pimientos

Instructions

1. Add hominy, grits, and water to rice cooker, and press Cook.
2. When on Warm setting, add pimento juice, spices, and cheese until cheese melts.

*D*ESSERTS

Gingerbread Cake

SERVINGS: 8
PREP TIME: 5 min.
TOTAL TIME: 1 hour 15 min.

Ingredients

- 1 1/2 cups white flour
- 1/4 cup sugar
- 1 teaspoon baking soda
- 1/4 teaspoon salt
- 1/2 teaspoon cinnamon
- 3 teaspoons ginger powder
- 1/3 cup oil
- 1/2 cup un-sulphured molasses
- 1 tablespoon vinegar
- 3/4 cup water

Instructions

1. Combine all dry ingredients well. Add oil, molasses, vinegar, and water in the same order. Stir batter until smooth, about 1 minute.
2. Oil or spray cooker spray inside of rice cooker bowl. Pour batter mix in rice cooker. Set to slow or regular cycle. If possible set timer for one hour. (Cooker will shut off after 5 minutes to Warm, restart to Cook cycle and 'bake' for about an hour or until a tooth pick comes out clean from middle of cake). Check progress at 45 minutes, since some rice cookers are faster than others. When toothpick comes clean, turn off.
3. Remove from rice cooker and allow cake to cool 15 minutes in bowl. After cooling put serving dish over top of the cooker bowl and quickly turn over. Transfer cake from bowl to serving dish.
4. Serve warm or cold, topped with puree from canned pears.

Rice Pudding

SERVINGS: 8
PREP TIME: 10 min.
TOTAL TIME: 40 min.

Ingredients

- 5 1/2 cups skim milk
- 2 cups short-grain white rice
- 1 cup white sugar
- 1/2 teaspoon ground cinnamon
- 2 1/2 cups skim milk

Instructions

1. Place 5 1/2 cups skim milk, rice, sugar, and cinnamon in a rice cooker. Stir to combine.
2. Cover and cook for one cycle in rice cooker until rice is creamy and tender, about 20 minutes.
3. Stir in remaining 2 1/2 cup milk.
4. Allow to cool before serving.

Coconut-Pecan Upside Down Cake

SERVINGS: 4
PREP TIME: 5 min.
TOTAL TIME: 45 min

Ingredients

- 1/2 cup butter, softened
- 1/2 cup dark brown sugar
- 1/2 cup shredded coconut
- 2/3 cup chopped pecans
- 1/2 cup semi-sweet chocolate
- 2 tablespoons milk
- 1 (9 ounce) box of yellow cake mix or 0.5 (18 1/4 ounce) box cake mix

Instructions

1. Melt butter in rice cooker. Spray with cooking spray or use parchment paper on bottom of pan. Combine brown sugar, coconut, pecan's and semi-sweet chocolates with a bit of milk. Spread over the butter. Mix up cake mix according to the directions on the box.
2. Hit Cook, it should take around 40 minutes. Turn off and wait a few minutes before removing the pan from the rice cooker.
3. Turn cake over and allow to cool before cutting.

Apple Rice Pudding

SERVINGS: 4
PREP TIME: 20 min.
TOTAL TIME: 40 min.

Ingredients

- 2 cups apples, peeled, cored, and diced
- 1 cup short-grain white rice
- 3 cups water
- 1/2 teaspoon salt
- 1 cup raisins
- 1 pinch nutmeg
- 1 (14 ounce) can sweetened condensed milk
- 4 tablespoons butter
- 1 1/2 tablespoons vanilla

Instructions

1. Put rice, salt, boiling water, raisins, apples, and nutmeg in rice cooker. Turn on to Cook setting. When it switches to Warm, stir in the condensed milk, vanilla, and butter. Turn on to Cook again.
2. Check pudding when it switches to Warm. Set to cook again if there is too much liquid.
3. Garnish with cinnamon.

Chocolate Cake

SERVINGS: 12
PREP TIME: 5 min.
TOTAL TIME: 1 hour 5 min

Ingredients

- 1 1/2 cups white flour
- 1/2 cup raw sugar
- 4 tablespoons dark cocoa
- 1 teaspoon baking soda
- 1/2 teaspoon salt
- 1/2 teaspoon cinnamon
- 1/4 teaspoon double-acting baking powder
- 90 ml sunflower oil
- 1/2 teaspoon vanilla
- 1 tablespoon vinegar
- 1 cup water

Instructions

1. Add and mix together the dry ingredients. Add wet ingredients to the mixture, mixing well until smooth, around 1 minute. Pour batter into the greased rice cooker bowl.
2. Set rice cooker to Slow for 60 minutes, if it doesn't have one just use the regular Cook cycle. If rice cooker goes to Warm cycle, allow to be in that mode for a few minutes then restart timer for remainder time to equal 60 minutes total cook time. Check at 45 minutes.
3. When a toothpick comes out clean from edges and center of cake, it is cooked.
4. Take bowl out when cake is finished, and allow to cool for 15 minutes. Remove cake by inverting bowl on serving plate.
5. Sprinkle with powdered sugar or top with your favourite frosting.

THANK YOU

Thank you for checking out the Quick and Easy Rice Cooker Meals Cookbook. I hope you enjoyed these recipes as much as I have. I am always looking for feedback on how to improve, so if you have any questions, suggestions, or comments please send me an email at susan.evans.author@gmail.com. Also, if you enjoyed the book would you consider leaving on honest review? As a new author, they help me out in a big way. Thanks again, and have fun cooking!

Check out more cookbooks:

Vegetarian Mediterranean Cookbook:
Over 50 recipes for appetizers, salads, dips, and main dishes

Quick & Easy Asian Vegetarian Cookbook:
Over 50 recipes for stir fries, rice, noodles, and appetizers

Vegetarian Slow Cooker Cookbook:
Over 75 recipes for meals, soups, stews, desserts, and sides

Quick & Easy Vegan Desserts Cookbook:
Over 80 delicious recipes for cakes, cupcakes, brownies, cookies, fudge, pies, candy, and so much more!

Quick & Easy Microwave Meals:
Over 50 recipes for breakfast, snacks, meals and desserts

Halloween Cookbook:
80 Ghoulish recipes for appetizers, meals, drinks, and desserts

Printed in Great Britain
by Amazon